Postcards from the Oregon Coast
History Presented by the People Who Lived It

Tillamook, Newport and Surrounding Communities 1905-1935

Bruce G. Walker

Mary E. Webster, editor

Post Cards From the Oregon Coast
History Presented by the People Who Lived It
Copyright 2018

Tillamook, Lincoln Counties, Oregon Coast

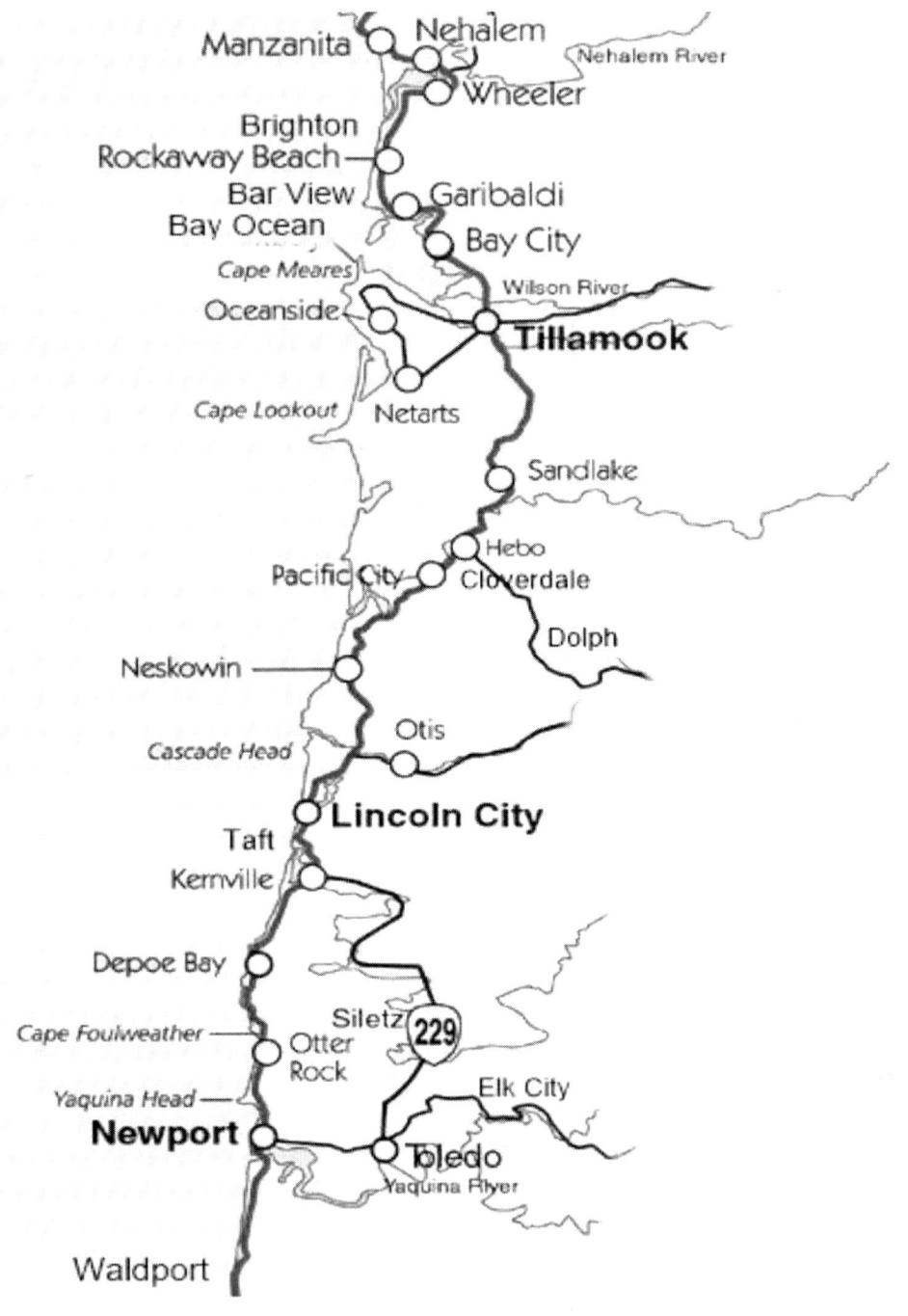

This book is dedicated to all people who were told they would be a failure, but succeeded anyway!

Other books edited by Mary E. Webster

The Federalist Papers: In Modern Language, 1999

The Federalist Papers: Modern English Edition Two, 2008

The Federalist Papers: Summaries of All 85 Papers, 2008

The United States Constitution: Annotated with The Federalist Papers in Modern English, 2010

The Federalist Papers: In Modern English: Compact Edition, 2012

Novels by Mary E. Webster

Swing Into Love, 1979

Love's Dark Wilderness, 1980

Love Storm, 1984

Introduction 1
Tillamook 2
Steamer Golden Gate..4
Early 20th Century in Tillamook, Lincoln Counties............................5
Trask Trail: Tillamook Road..6
Logging, Tillamook, 1905..9
Basketball, Tillamook, February 1909...10
Church Party, Tillamook..11
Tillamook, October 1908 12
Tillamook, The Teen Years..13
Looking West on Main Street, Tillamook..14
Close Up 18
1918 19
Close Up 19
"Tillamook" Gasoline Engine Ship..20
The Della, Cape Lookout State Park 21
Train Travel Comes to Tillamook, 1911 22
Tillamook, 1911 23
Tillamook, 1911 24
Tillamook, 1913 26
"Canned" 1914 28
Business Street, Tillamook...29
Looking west. Note the concrete sidewalks. 29
Second Street, Tillamook 30
Tillamook High School Basketball Team 1933 31
Tillamook, October 1917 32
Bay Ocean 34
Natatorium, Bay Ocean, 1914..35
Bay City, December 2, 1911 36
The Yacht Bay Ocean...36
Bay City...38
Dr. Hawk..38
Bay City, October 3, 1908..40
Bay City, August 18, 1912 42
A Brighton fire documented...44
Oceanside, November 25, 1936 45
Rockaway, 1914 46
Rockaway, 1920s..48

Rockaway, 1934	48
Rockaway, August 3, 1920	49
Rockaway, The Fire of 1934	50
Rockaway, 1933-1935	52
Rockaway, 1935	53
Netarts, 1915	54
Netarts, Happy Camp, 1920s	56
Garibaldi	56
Bar View	58
Bar View Beach, August 24, 1910	60
Bar View, 1918	61
Lifesaving Stations	62
Wreck of the Mimi, February 1913	66
Garibaldi Rescue, April 6, 1913	67
The Wreck of the Glenneslin	68
Cloverdale	70
Dolph, 1915	72
Pacific City	73
Nehalem	74
Nehalem, April 27, 1928	76
Wheeler	77
Spruce Brigades	78
Spruce Brigade loading rail cars near Tillamook	80
Taft	83
Grahams Landing/Toledo	84
Toledo Football, around 1916-1918	86
Newport, 1905	88
Newport, 1906	89
Newport, Front Street, 1910	90
Nye Beach 1918	94
Abbey Hotel, Newport	97
Gas Schooner Anvil	100
Train Travel to Newport	102
Blakley Family, Newport, Postcards	104
Newport, July 26, 1916	106
Newport	108
Elk City	110
Waldport Camp	112
Waldport	114
Epilogue	117

Introduction

This book was put together to give you a glimpse into life on the Central Oregon coast in the early years of the twentieth century. I focused on Tillamook, Newport, and surrounding communities.

Most of the images are from real picture postcards, or RPPC's. And there are a few family photographs. RPPC's recorded both local historical events and mundane, everyday occurrences, and could be sent anywhere in the world. My earliest images start at 1905 and end about 1935, just as access to the coastal regions became easier.

Spend time looking at the images. One-hundred years is not so long ago, since the average life expectancy is seventy-plus years.

The correspondence on the back of the cards is presented as written, without corrections. It provides the human connection to a way of life that we have forgotten. Self-reliance was expected of everyone. Time was less of a problem because, like it or not, nothing moved faster than a horse.

When the train made it through the coast range, everything changed. People came overland in droves! With the arrival of the automobile, the pace of life quickened. However, the effect was delayed because the roads had to be improved before the automobile could be relied on. A horse never got flats, nor did trains. The coastal roads were hard on rubber tires.

Now, one-hundred years later, the coast has gone through many changes. However, nothing is as it was supposed to be. The authorities in Newport did not want a railroad terminal. Newport was supposed to become like San Francisco, but the railroad traveled only as far as Yaquina. Today, Lincoln County, where Newport is located, has approximately 45,000 citizens. It's growing but it's no San Francisco.

Tillamook was supposed to boom to over 20,000 people. Well, it didn't happen—unless you count cows in the population mix! In 2018, there are 22,000 cows in the greater Tillamook area with a population of 5,000 citizens in that same area. The population of the entire county is 25,000.

Most people either love or hate the coastal weather. People who love it, often find a way to live here. People who hate it, find a way to vacation here when the valley heat drives them to the coast for relief.

Tillamook

*If you ever come to Tillamook on a boat, here is where you'll land.
With love to all   Ellen Bewley*

Steamer Golden Gate

The Golden Gate was a passenger and freight steamer that replaced the Argo that wrecked at Tillamook in 1908. She held 40 passengers and all necessary lifesaving equipment. She served Tillamook, Astoria, and other small harbors.

Mrs. B. C. Lamb
489 E 39th St.
Portland Ore
Dear Mother,
Your two towels came. We are all well and lonesome.
Charles

Early 20th Century in Tillamook, Lincoln Counties

In 1909, life expectancy was 47 years, 14% of homes had a bathtub, and only 8% had a telephone. The average worker made between $200 and $400 per year—if you didn't die of pneumonia or the flu or tuberculosis or diarrhea! Only 8,000 people had a car in the whole country. Only 6% of students graduated high school. 20% of adults couldn't read or write.

In fact, 90% of doctors didn't go to college, they attended "medical schools" and most were condemned as substandard by government. Most "medical cures" consisted of narcotics, and heroin was touted as a perfect guardian of health. There were a lot of addicts, mostly women because they couldn't go to the local bar for a drink, so they took "remedies" for relief. Cocaine was sold as a hair tonic. More than a few sick children were overdosed by these "remedies, cures, purifiers, tonics, and extracts."

Women only washed their hair once a month, using eggs or borax.

Our northern neighbor, Canada, passed a law banning poor people from entering the country for any reason.

Trask Trail: Tillamook Road

There was a time when the adage, "you can't get there from here" was an accurate truism about Tillamook. For a long time, the Trask Trail was the only overland route to Tillamook. It cut through the very rough terrain of the Northern Oregon Coast Range mountains.

Sometimes the mail could only be walked in once a week, by some poor guy in snow shoes. It was a miserable two-day journey in an open wagon with the risk of getting soaked in a downpour or riding through a cold, wet fog.

Some travelers carried side arms, as demonstrated in the picture on the next page.

Tillamook Road

Tillamook Road

Before 1906, messages had to be written on the front of the card.

Logging, Tillamook, 1905

Basketball, Tillamook, February 1909

In late 1891, Dr. James Naismith invented basketball. It shared a name and some basic rules of the modern game. Basketball underwent epic evolutions over the years. The first games were 9-on-9, used closed peach baskets hung at each end of the gym, and used a soccer ball. The first "official" game ended with a score of 1-0!

Basketball quickly became a popular indoor sport around the world. By the early 1900's, many YMCAs, high schools, and colleges had teams. There were even professional leagues. There were five players per team, set shots, chest passes, and rudimentary offensive and defensive strategies. The introduction of dribbling changed the game forever. Amazingly, basketball was a medal sport at the 1904 Olympics.

Ruby Sadd, Portland, Oregon
I suppose you think I had forgotten you. Well, I haven't but I feel ashamed of myself for not answering sooner.
This is our Basketball team. I suppose you know the fellow standing at the right. Robt. Stillwell

The note on the front of the card is written by the coach.

Church Party, Tillamook

The pioneer family of Thomas Stillwell arrived in Tillamook in 1861. They laid out the town and opened the first store. A street is named after him.

Chas Lamb
City
Party at the church Thursday evening.
Come out.
E.H.

This card (and a couple other cards) was purchased from the Lamb family estate.

11

Tillamook, October 1908

Your mother Mrs. M. A. Kimball

Well Dear son I received your card and letter and will write to you in a few days this a view looking from the academy towards the school house down in front of Frank old place but it looks like it is on the obsite side of the street we have a case of small pox in town the Laundryman has it and he don't now where he got it only in cloths this will be all write soon good by

Tillamook, The Teen Years

This view of Tillamook was taken by *T. R. Monk Photographer Tillamook Ore.* Look carefully and you will see it's a combination of two negatives artfully butted up to each other to create the panoramic image.

The Allen House is the featured structure. It was the favored gathering spot in Tillamook for social events and conducting business. It had 24 rooms, a large dining room, and kitchen. The large amount of wood piled behind the hotel was for the kitchen wood stoves.

Looking West

13

Looking West on Main Street, Tillamook

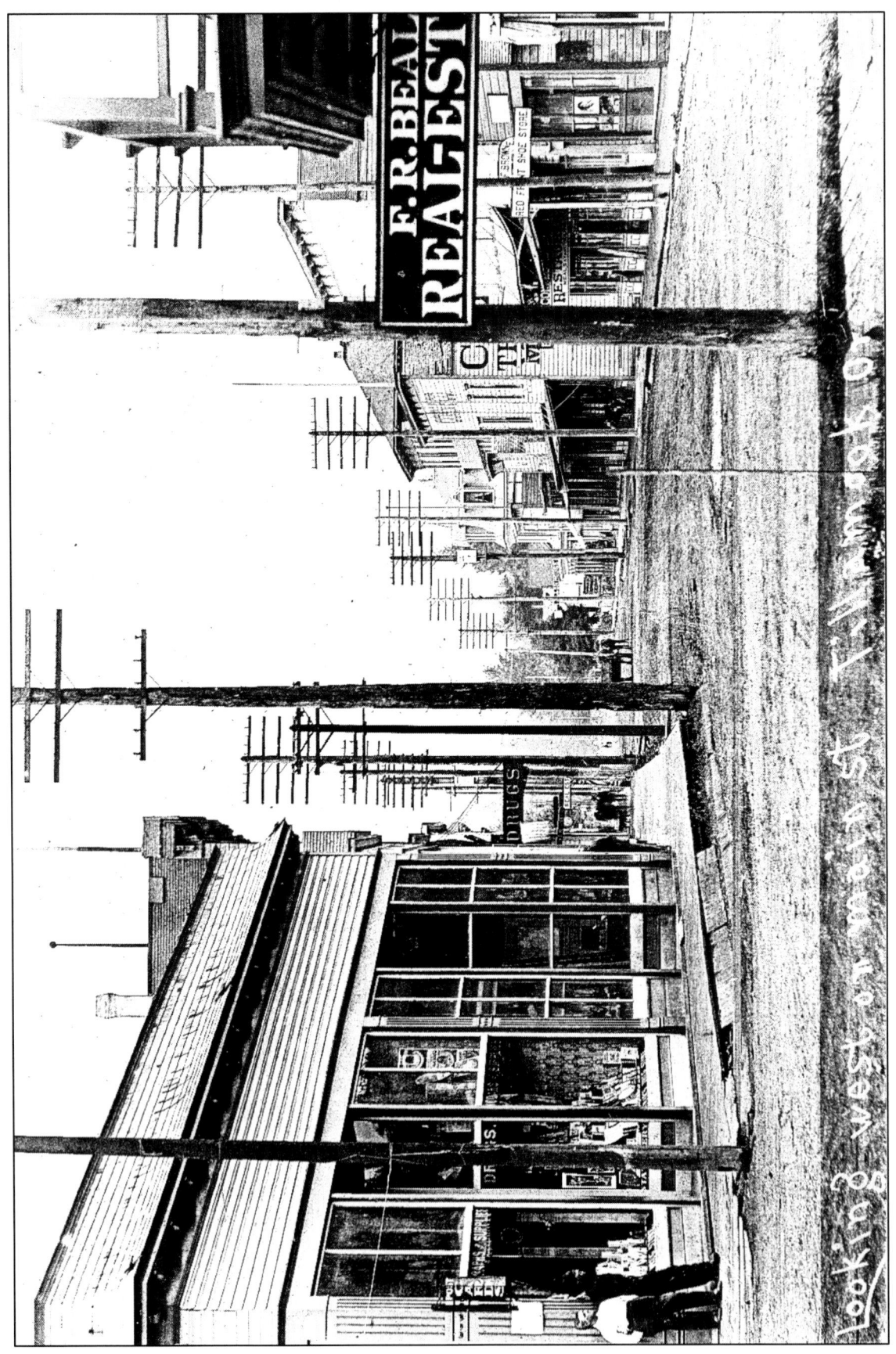

Close Up

1918

Close Up

19

"Tillamook" Gasoline Engine Ship

The Della, Cape Lookout State Park

Train Travel Comes to Tillamook, 1911

The construction of the railroad from Portland to Tillamook began in June of 1906 by the Pacific Railway and Navigation Company. According to this image, the first Portland to Tillamook service was on October 9, 1911. This was the critical first step in ending Tillamook County's isolation from the rest of the world. By 1918, the county was well connected by rail, opening up what would be many popular tourist destinations. It was no longer necessary to risk a lengthy boat ride, with all of its potential discomforts and hazards in an ocean-going steamer, or a very uncomfortable two-day trip over the Trask Trail.

Tillamook, 1911

Friday July 20-11

Dear Mama &

We're going to the country with the club to stay all day today. This is where I live. In the garage where the dots are. 2 rooms. Will write a letter tomorrow we are both O.K.

Looking West

Tillamook, 1911

Miss Kittie Shyer
Kansas

Dear Girlie:
Please do not think I have forgotten about you for I have done nothing
of the kind & sometime I will make up for this neglect. Had about 6
in of snow and enjoyed it very much. Is raining now K.

These boats were known as the Butterfly Fishing Fleet

May 30, 1912
Am taking in Tillomook will be up before long be shure and send that
Phonagraph   Mury   (T.R. Monk photograph)

Tillamook, 1913

Miss W. Pettys
6503 Whitman Ave.
Portland Ore.
Feb 3/ We are still working on this mail
Dear Loraine
Received some Sentinel today in this bunch of delayed mail which I think came from you. And work & thank you very very much. They were just what I wanted with much love to you all
From matr.

Tillamook, Oreg Feb 4, 7AM 1913

Close Up

Five tons Mail brought from Portland to Tillamook by Capt. Jenkins on the Herrie D. # Feb. 1st 1913.

"Canned" 1914

These high school boys were expelled for stealing women's underwear from the domestic arts classroom.

From the Monk Studio

Business Street, Tillamook
Looking west. Note the concrete sidewalks.

Second Street, Tillamook

The Todd Hotel, which became infamous when materials from the KKK was found during its demolition.

Tillamook High School Basketball Team 1933

"B" Squad
(Top Row) left to right: Griffen, Hedeger, Mueller, Wagy, Plank
(Center Row) Philllips, Goddard, Steidegar, Giddings, Sissik, Koch, Miller
(Front Row) Effenburger, Hines, Baumgartner, Eason, Walker

Tillamook, October 1917

Mrs. E.W. Black
Albany
Oregon Route 3.

I will write a letter tomarow night
Dear mother
Was glad to get the card nana was in Tillamook for a short visit. I saw her. All four of uncle Geoges children have to-main poison cause from cheese they are some better

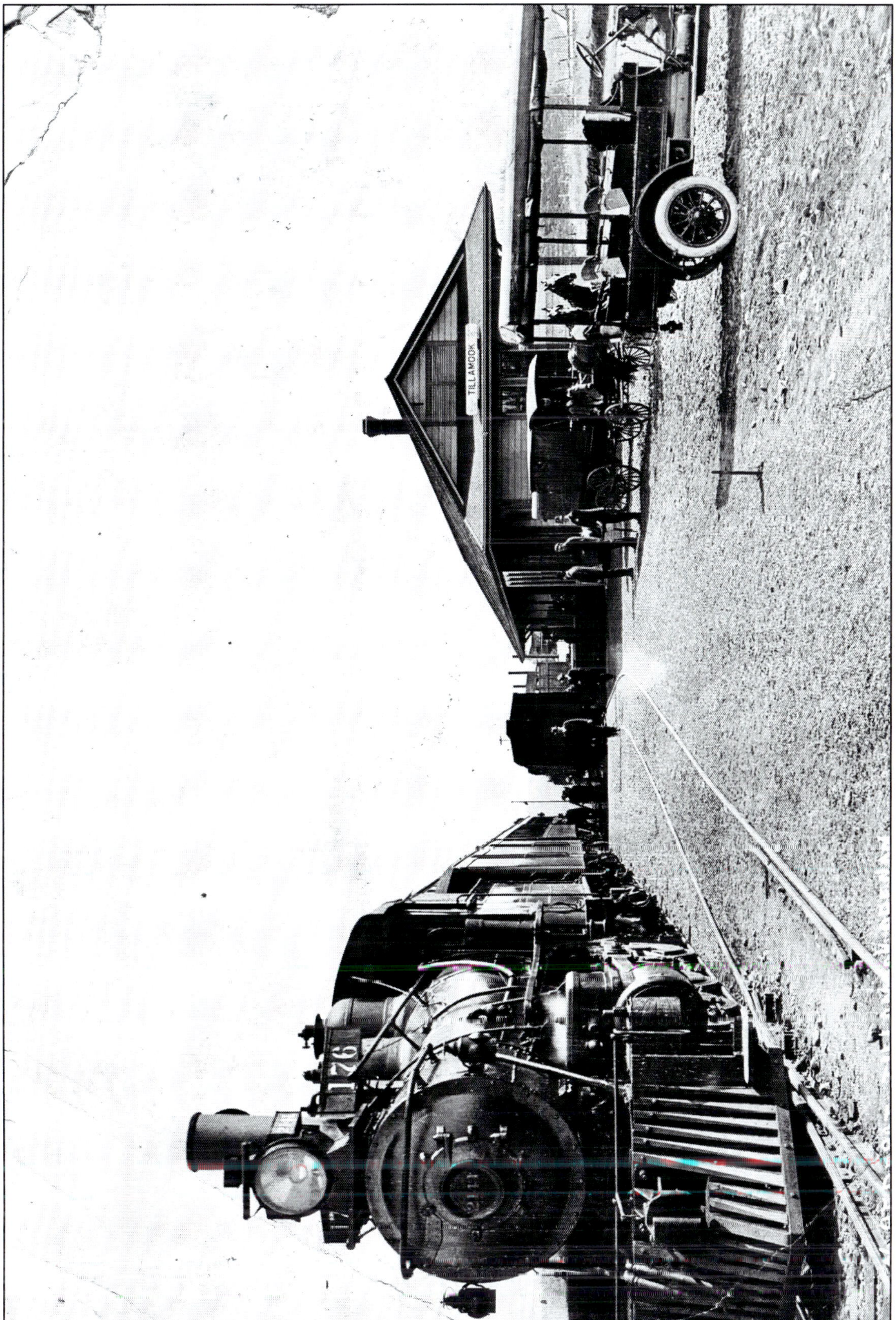

Bay Ocean

While hunting and sightseeing, T. I. Potter discovered the area that would become Bay Ocean. He purchased the land with his father/business partner, Thomas Benton Potter. Bay Ocean was founded in 1906. A post office was established in 1909. In 1914, the population was 2,000. Tourism fueled its economy. The town had a diesel power plant, a telephone system, a 1,000-seat theater, a shooting range, a Texaco gas station, a dance hall, and a natatorium with a wave-making machine and an orchestra to entertain the swimmers.

There was no overland access to Bay Ocean. Both building materials and people were brought in by boat. A small narrow-gauge railroad was built on the beach to haul materials. The track was slid over the sand as needed.

Bay Ocean's residents wanted a jetty to smooth out the ocean's waves. The Army Corp of engineers recommended two jetties, which would cost $2.2 million. Thinking this cost too much, the town had had only the north jetty built at a cost of $800,000 with Bay Ocean's citizens paying half. This decision doomed Bay Ocean. The Pacific Ocean reclaimed the land. There is no longer any trace of what was once Bay Ocean.

Natatorium, Bay Ocean, 1914

Bay City, December 2, 1911

Miss Nanea Kunz
Titusville
Penn'a
R.D. #79

Dear Nea:
Our house stands at the bend of the road with those trees in the front yard. I sprained my ankle again yesterday it is quite lame.
What are you going to do xmas?
Our mail comes on the RR. Now
Ans soon Dora

The Yacht Bay Ocean

This photo shows the yacht Bay Ocean, moored at Bay City. This was the largest yacht on the west coast at the time and weighed 148 tons. It was used to transport people from Portland to the resort town of Bay Ocean, a three-day trip. The Bay Ocean was built in Portland, Oregon, in 1911. The yacht was acquired by the Navy in June, 1918, then decommissioned in 1919, and sold in 1921.

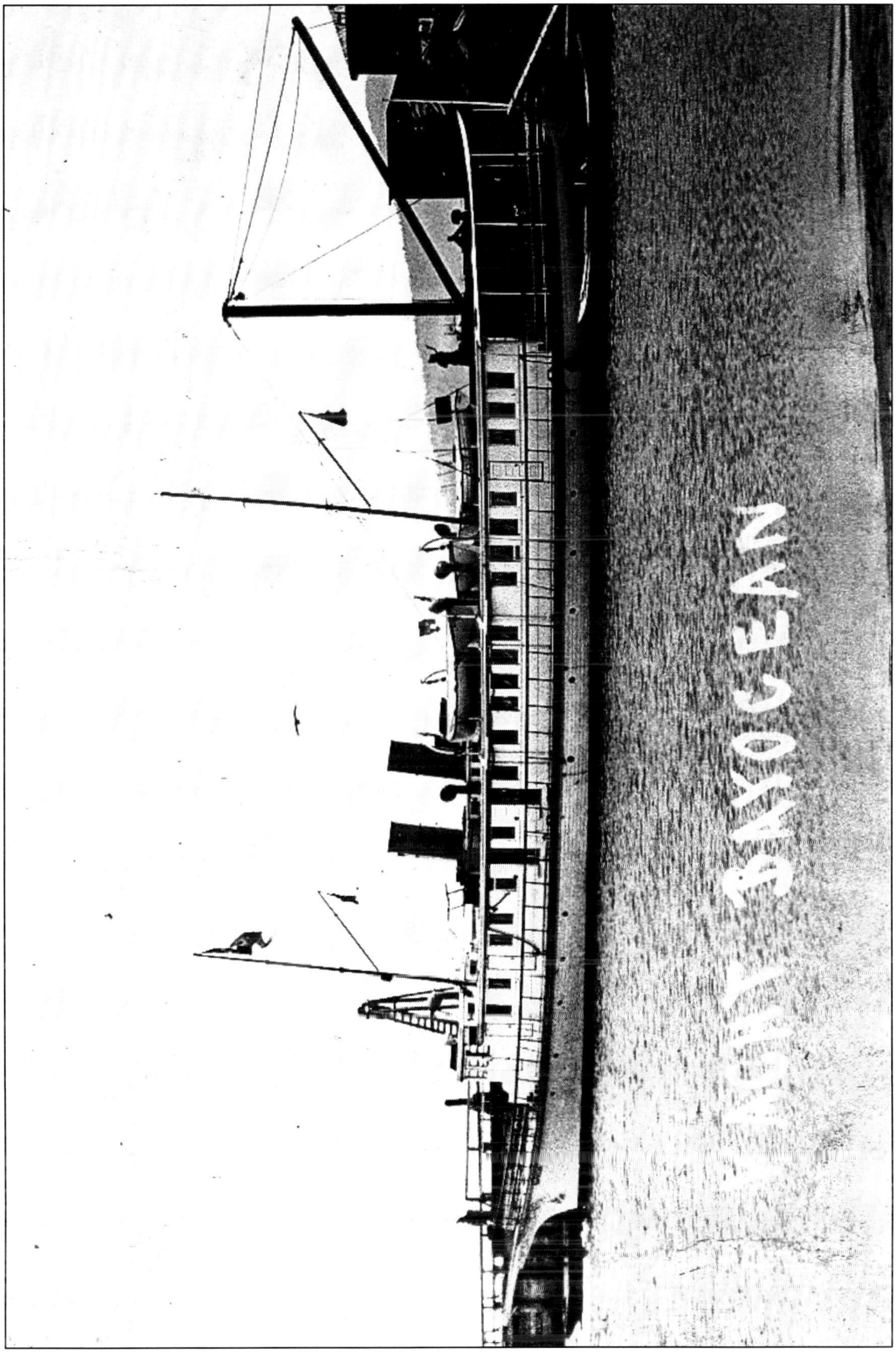

Bay City

Brothers John O. and Scott Bozorth published a promotional brochure in 1914, which gave some outlandish descriptions of the glories of Bay City and the surrounding area. Bozorth describes the water system, which he owned, as having "a capacity to supply 6,000 people…The water is of excellent purity, and is equal to Bull Run water. The Bay City Land Company has acquired Sugar Loaf Mountain, just east of the city, on which it intends to have a stand pipe. This will give immense pressure in case of fire. Sugar Loaf Mountain is about 400 feet high and contains about forty acres. Its symmetrical beauty is enhanced by the more distant mountains as a background. The company owns water rights on the Wilson River. This capacity will be sufficient to supply 150,000 people. Thus BAY CITY is assured of absolutely pure water."

Most of downtown Bay City burned to the ground, chiefly because the fire department couldn't get enough water pressure to get water onto the fire. So much for honesty in advertising.

Dr. Hawk

Dr. Hawk was in Tombstone the day of the gunfight at the OK Corral, which may have given him the idea to move west. He and his family settled in Jefferson, near Salem, Oregon. In 1905, he traveled to Tillamook County, and purchased property in Bay City. In 1907, he and his family moved, traveling 120 miles in six days to reach Tillamook. Then he went on to Bay City, where he started his medical practice.

In 1908, Dr. Hawk began construction of a hospital. It took great ambition and a strong back to build an 80-room, multi-story hospital in an age of hand tools. It was an impressive structure. In 1918, during the flu pandemic, he cared for 1,500 flu patients—and none died!

In 1910, he became a member of the first board of commissioners for the port of Bay City. Later, he and a partner bought an old homestead five miles north of Geribaldi, subdivided it into 50 by 70 foot lots, and called it Rockaway Beach.

In 1922, Dr. Hawk and his wife were killed in an auto accident by a drunk driver while traveling through Hebo, Oregon. With no Dr. Hawk, the hospital closed. The hospital was used as a sanitarium and a hotel for a while, but its ultimate demise has been obscured by the fog of time.

[Information from articles by John R. Sollman.]

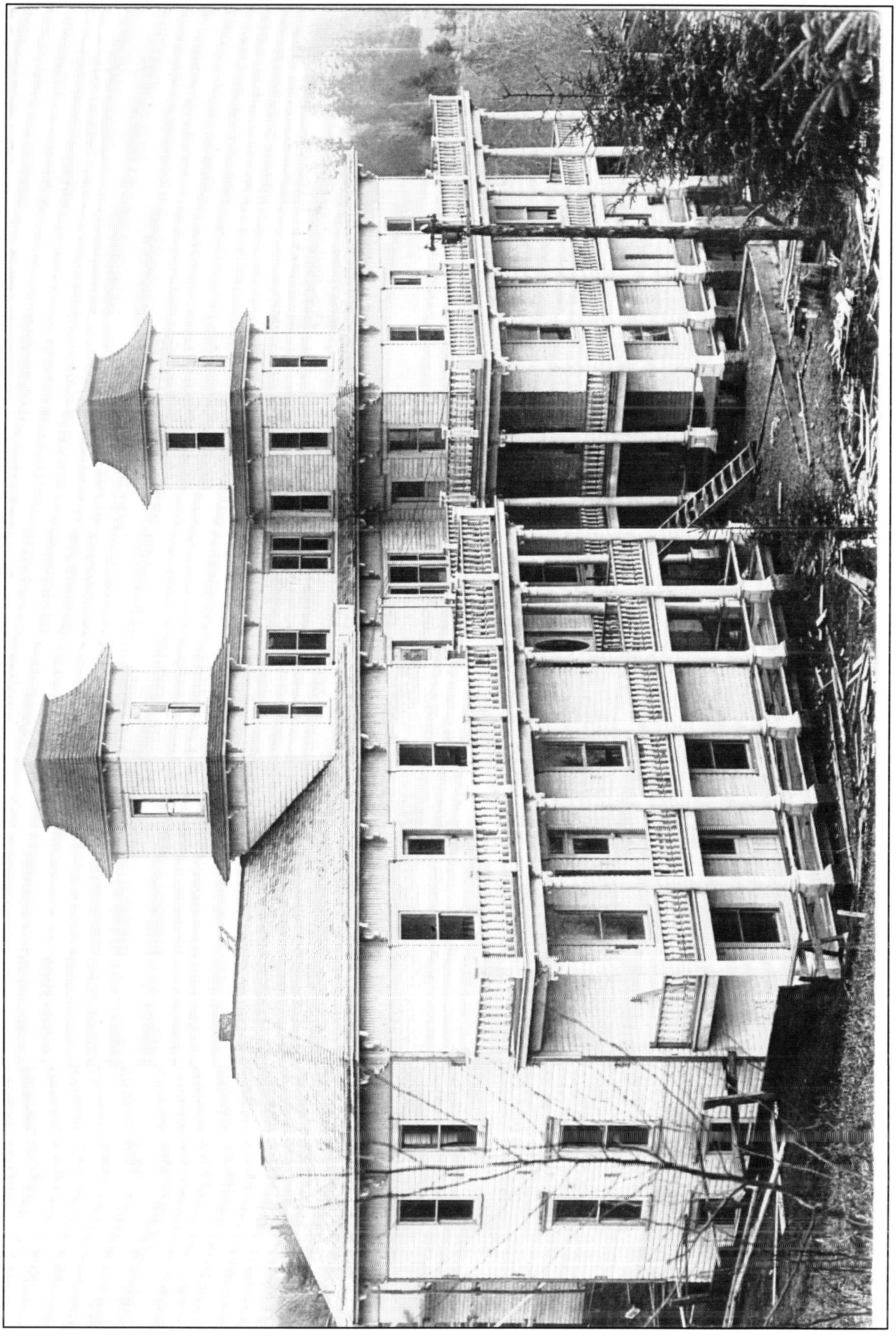

Bay City, October 3, 1908

Hello did you say to take a little lemon and I wouldn't be sick. Well I handed someone else the lemon. I was down and out after the first lunge and feel like rock a bye baby this morning. Will write in a few days love Zilda

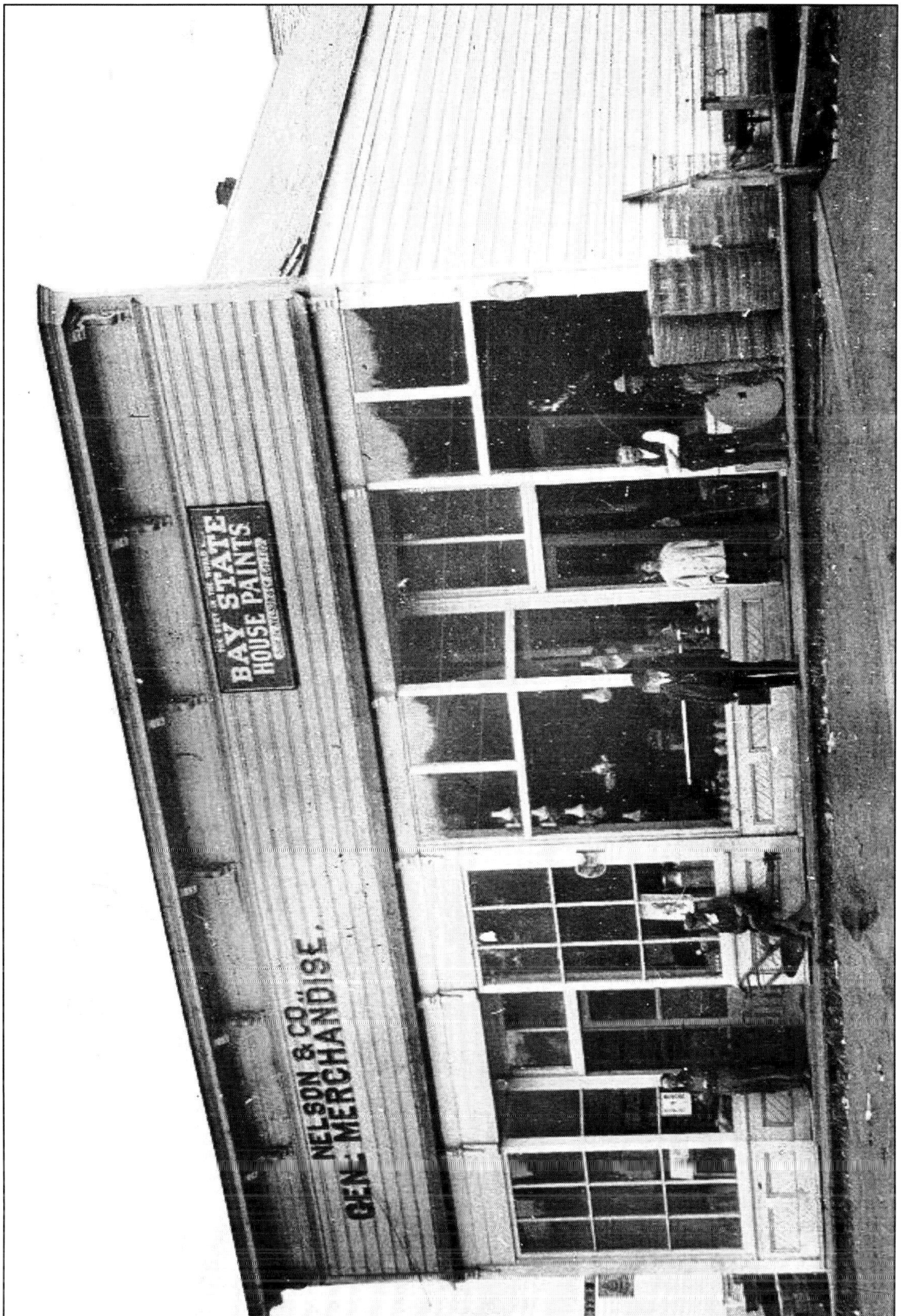
NELSON & CO.
GEN. MERCHANDISE
BAY STATE
HOUSE PAINTS

Bay City, August 18, 1912

Dear frend Gallagher we are out at sea side having a fine time might give yous a call before we go back to work

A lot of the photos (Real Picture Postcards) have a pole in the middle of the picture. I believe this was done on purpose to highlight that the towns had electricity.

4TH STREET LOOKING NORTH BAY CITY ORE

42

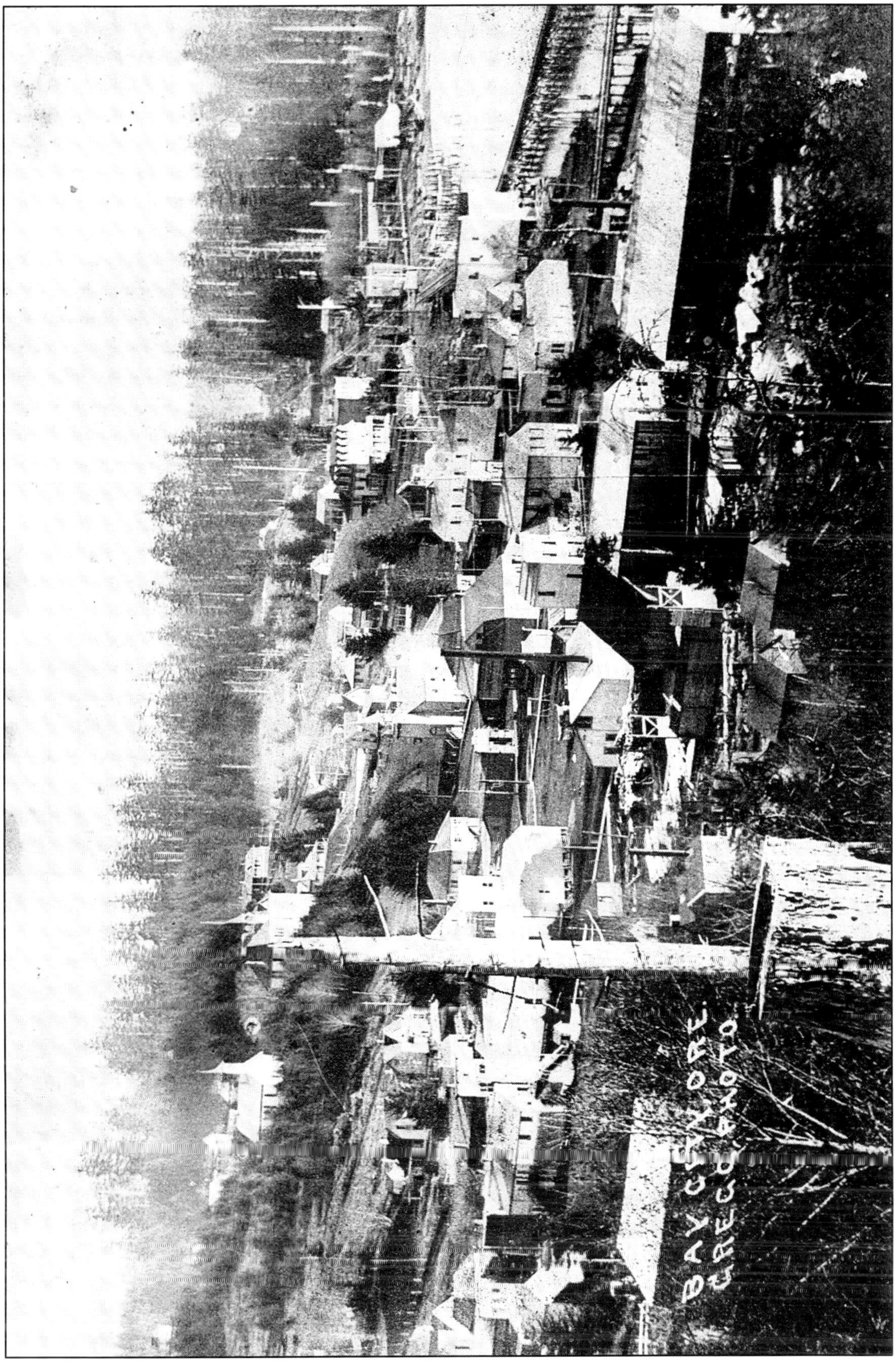

A Brighton fire documented

The house marked with an X is the ones that dident burn No=1=is the store. No=2= the three story bunk house where the fire started no=3=the pool hall & dance hall & Picture shoe combined no=4= the office. No 5 the laundry also a family lived in it, no=6= the hotel kitchen, no=7=is where we live you can see how close we were. And it sure came all most going the rest of the houses you can see are where people live.

44

Oceanside, November 25, 1936

"Resort town of Oceanside, nine miles west of Tillamook, saved from destruction last night, only by a shift of wind from north-east to north-west. A bad brush fire raged through the hills in the upper center of the picture. It reached the first curve from the bridge on the road in the upper right-hand corner." [News article.]

Rockaway, 1914

Monday July 28, 1914

Good afternoon: Have been out watching the bathers are going to see the train come in now all packed to leave at 5:36. Picture of Alfred, Reid, Estelle, Frank. X our house lots of new housing in Rockaway & along beach resorts—all strange people today-(as usual) old men, kids, women + children it is warm.
As ever Grace

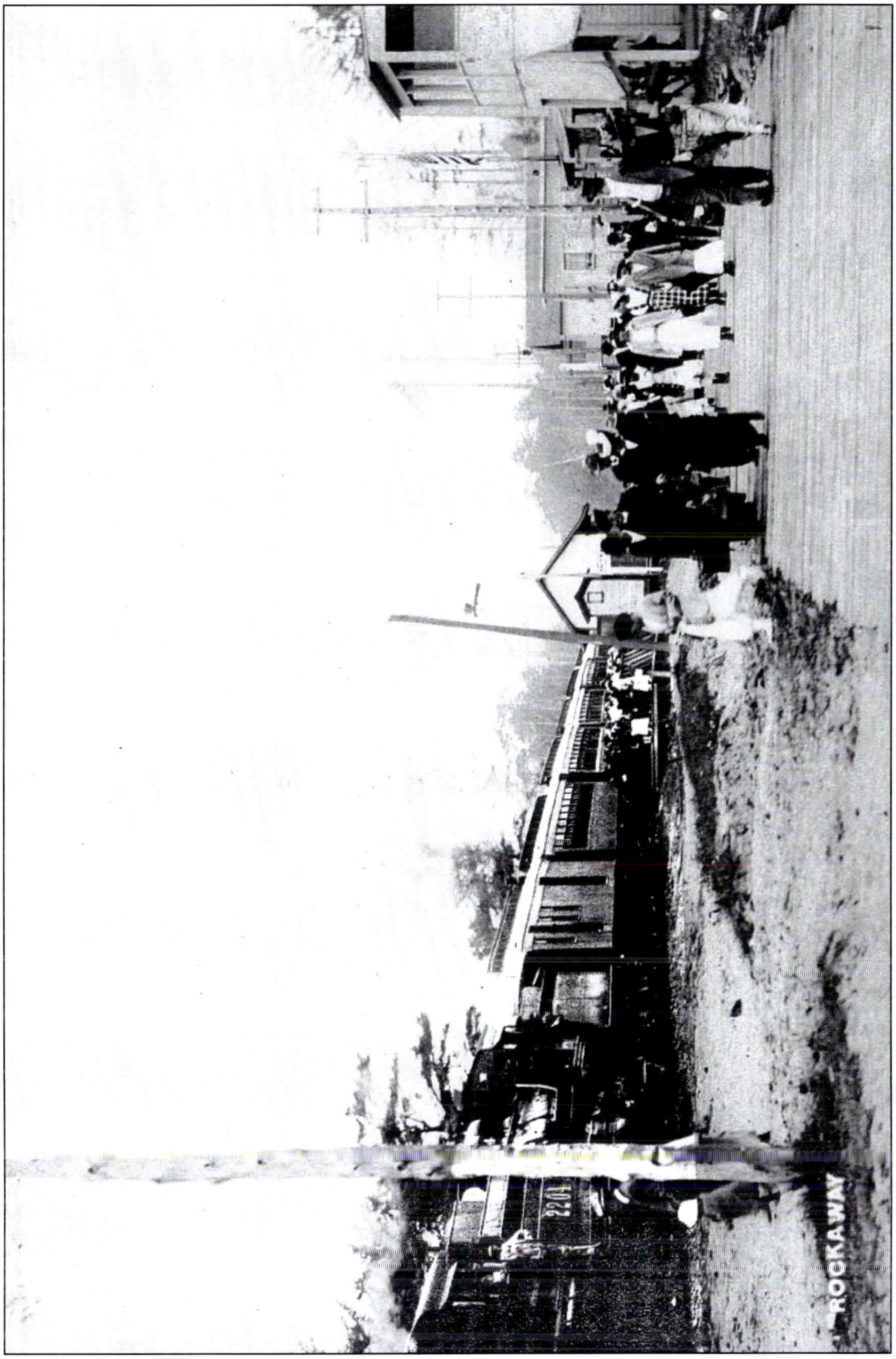
ROCKAWAY
2204

Rockaway, 1920s

Rockaway, 1934

Rockaway, August 3, 1920

Mrs. E H Otey
1132 E 28st N
Portland Ore

Dear Pa & Ma – Ganded
At 4 PM (Gorebbi) ? came back to Rockaway have a fine camping place plenty of wood and water and about 200 yards from the beach under shade trees, lots of campin here will write again

Actually, playing on logs in the surf is incredibly dangerous. Even 100 years later, people continue to die trying to do it.

49

Rockaway, The Fire of 1934

In the 1930's, my grandmother and mother, who lived in Portland, were regular visitors to Rockaway. My grandmother managed a group of cottages with the help of my mother, Frances. Mom also helped a couple run their horseback riding on the beach business. Tillamook County and Rockaway, in particular, became very popular in my parents' ethnic community.

Fire was a problem for the small towns in Tillamook County. The postcard on the opposite page documents the damage done to Rockaway. My Mom told me that at one time downtown Rockaway burnt down. I was very young and didn't believe her because my little-boy brain couldn't accept something like that could happen.

Fire photo is on the opposite page.

My mother, Frances George, is pictured on the far left.

Fire at Rockaway Aug 31-1934

Rockaway, 1933-1935

My mother, Frances George, is pictured on the far right.

Grandmother George with Frances

Frances with brother, sister.

Rockaway, 1935

A bathing beauty contest was held in 1935 in Rockaway. My mother, Frances George, is the second girl from the left with a sash that reads, "Miss Germany." Mom was just fifteen at the time. She told me that she didn't win.

Netarts, 1915

Mr. Ernest Belcher
Storm Lake, Iowa

We are on the coast once more. We finished our 85 mile wagon trip last night. It took us 2 full days it certainly is fun go camping especially out in wilderness in the woods up in the mountains. We're going bathing this afternoon.
Lovingly Henry and Meta—?

NO 17 CAMP AT NETARTS BEACH NEAR TILLAMOOK ORE

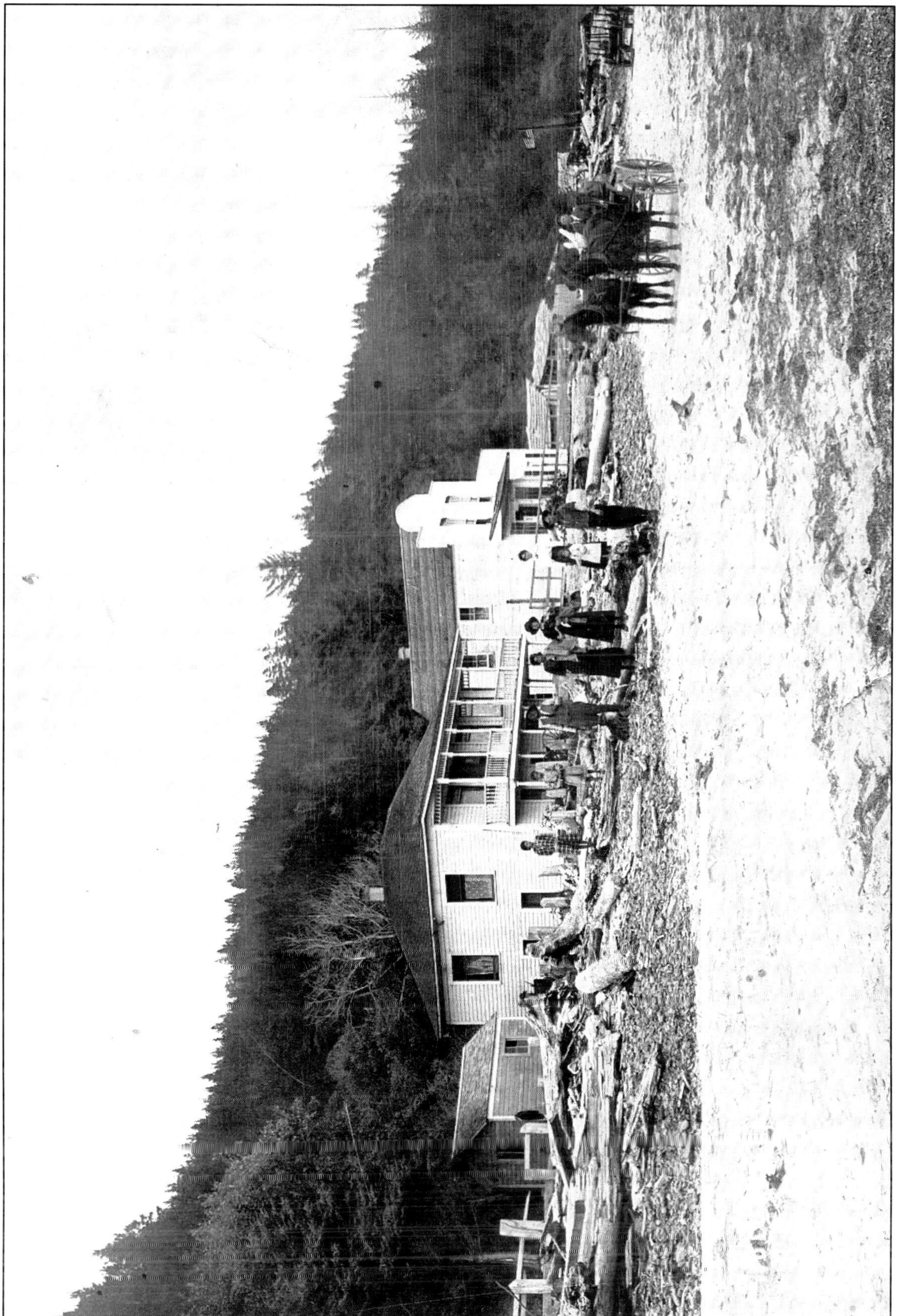

Netarts, Happy Camp, 1920s

Garibaldi

Dear Children— I have been looking in vain for a word from you but I shall continue to write until you say quite. I know there must be some good and sufficient reason. Katie will be in Portland for next week— from Hubbard. She has no hand to go around so you may not see her love all.

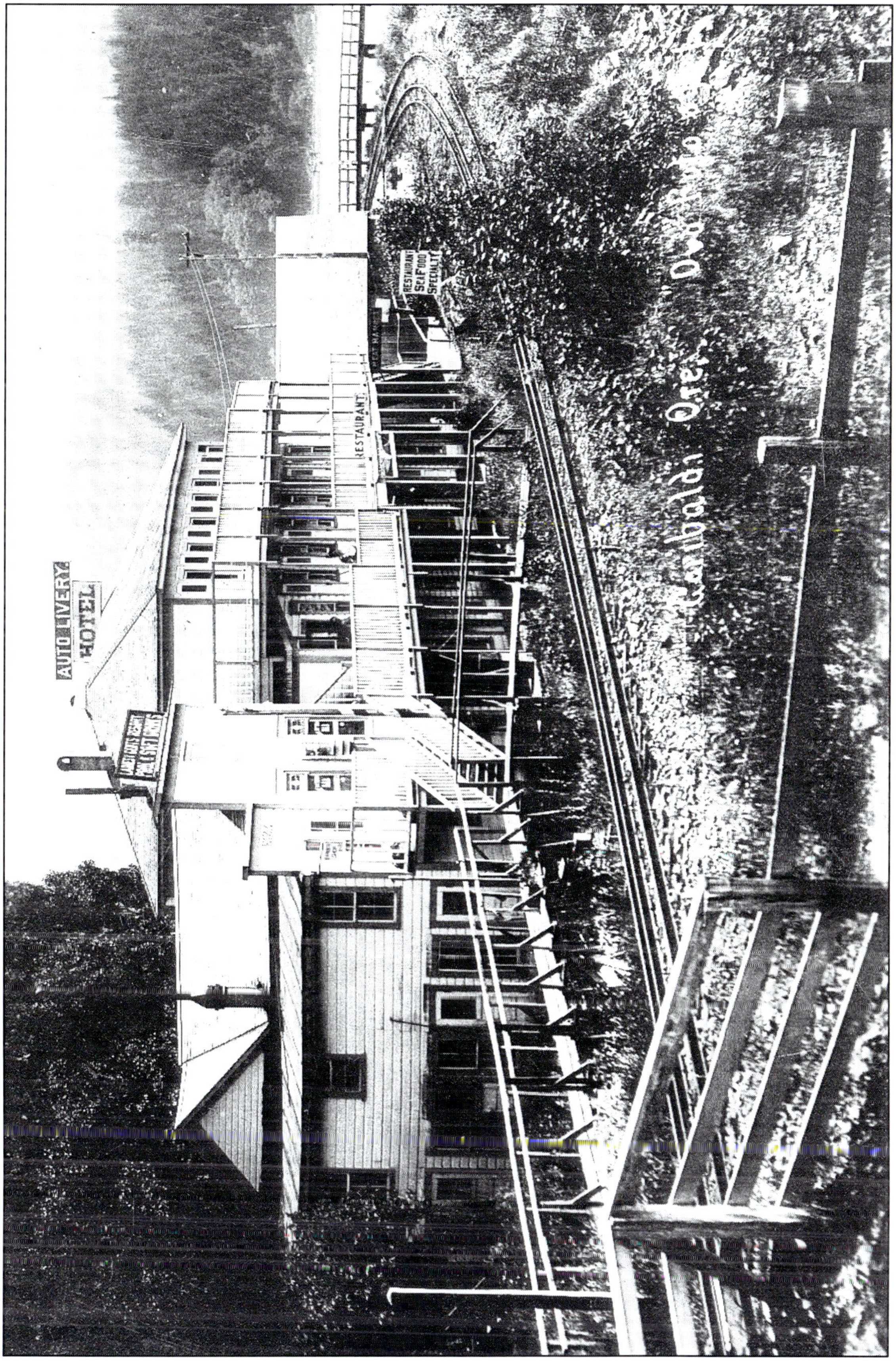
AUTO LIVERY
HOTEL
RESTAURANT

Bar View

In this image you have a model-T Ford on a dirt road and two people looking out over the water. Everyone is wearing an Army uniform. The Spruce Brigades (Army Signal Corp) vehicle of choice for transportation around the county was the Ford Model-T. as it was simple to operate and reliable for its day.

In the center of the image are the railroad tracks used to haul both tourists and the large boulders used for the construction of the north jetty. At that time, the lifesaving station was located at Bar View, built in 1908. It was abandoned and transferred to public ownership during World War II. The Garibaldi life-saving station is still in use as an active Coast Guard station.

Bar View, was and is a popular destination for camping and sightseeing.

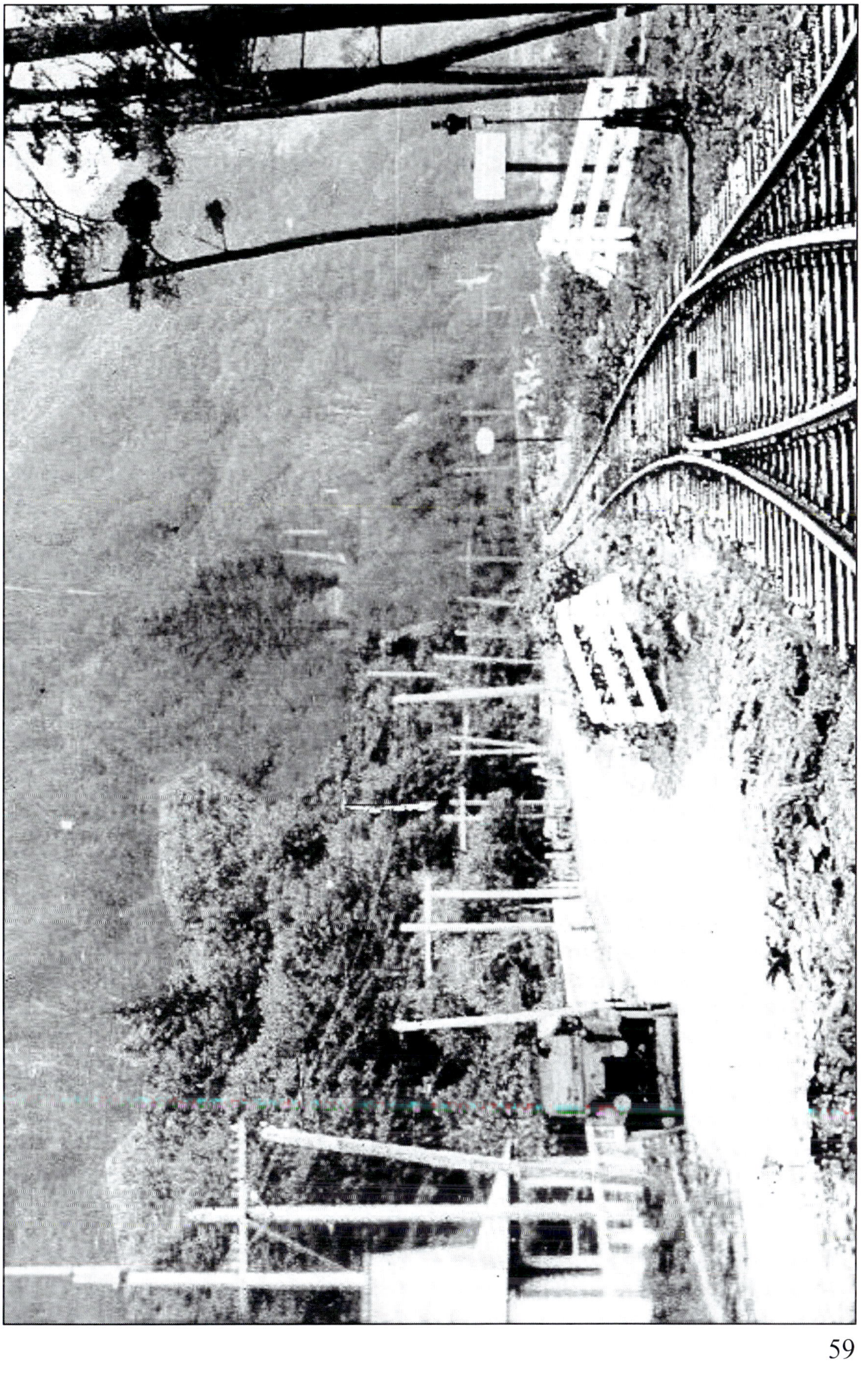

Bar View Beach, August 24, 1910

Mrs C. E. Hall
474 Alder Str.
Portland Oregon

Hello! Mom
I was in the surf Yesterday for the first time. We had a great time.
Be home soon
Edd & Flo.

Bar View, 1918

Mrs. Goodrich
Carlton Ore.

On this card is the house we rented, second house in wright hand row you can't see there in the other view they are still north up the railroad.

Lifesaving Stations

Lifesaving stations were located up and down the coast with Tillamook and Newport being no exception. Tillamook's lifesaving station was located in the town of Bar View, on Tillamook Bay. The Yaquina lifesaving station was in Newport.

"The stations of the Service fell into three categories: lifesaving, lifeboat, and houses of refuge. Lifesaving stations were manned by full-time crews during the period when wrecks were most likely this was known as the active season. By 1900, the active season was year-round. Most stations were in isolated areas and crewmen had to perform open beach launchings. That is, they were required to launch their boats from the beach into the surf. Before 1900, there were very few recreational boaters and most assistance cases came from ships engaged in commerce. Nearly all lifeboat stations were located at or near port cities. Here, deep water, combined with piers and other waterfront structures, allowed launching heavy lifeboats directly into the water by inclined ramps." [Wikipedia]

The lifesaving stations were incorporated into the Coast Guard in 1915.

U.S. Life saving Station, Garibaldi, Ore.

"U.S. Life-Savers"
Newport, Ore.

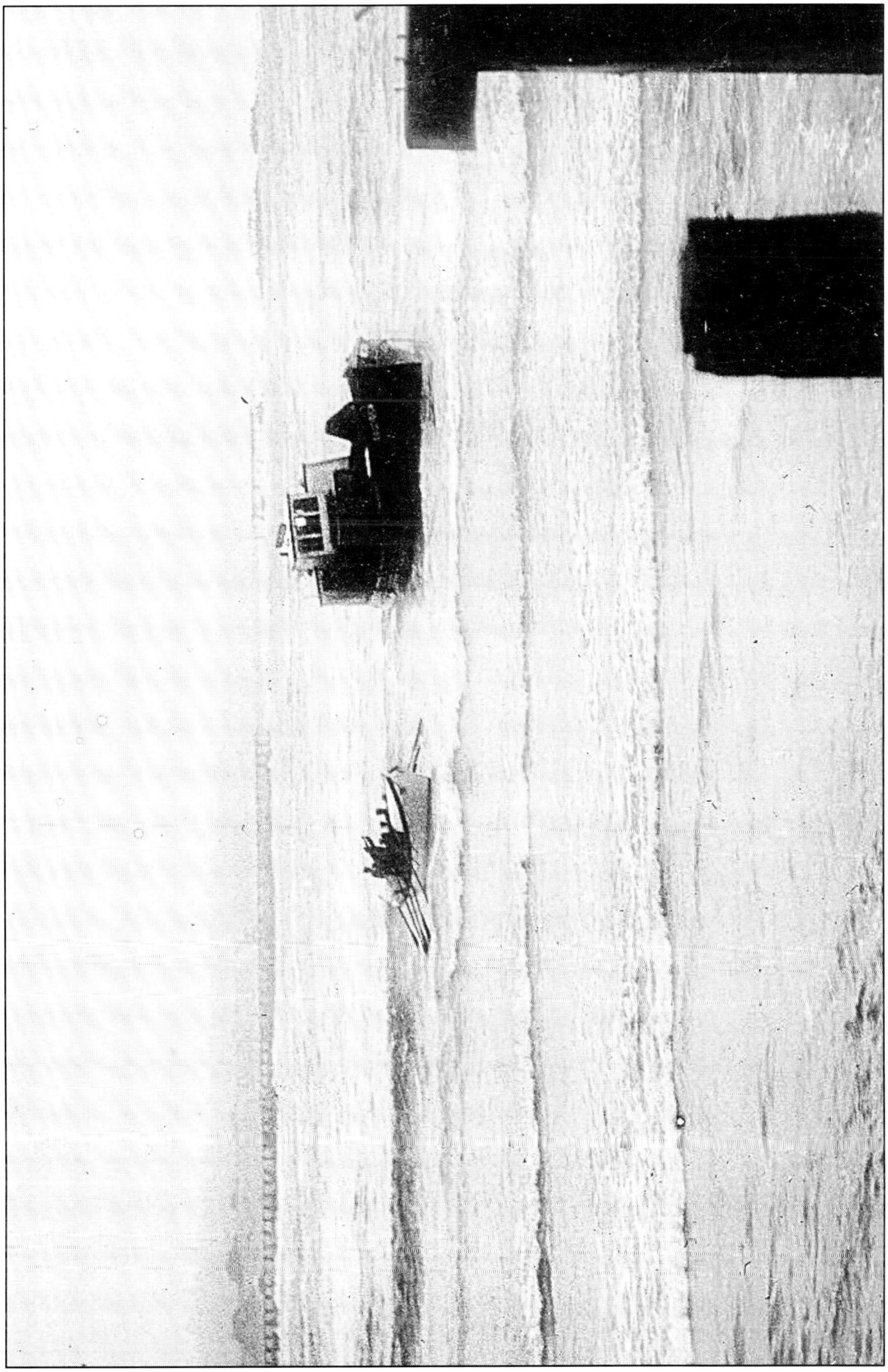

Wreck of the Mimi, February 1913

The Mimi, an iron hulled sailing ship built in 1893 in Germany, ran aground north of Nehalem because of dense fog. At low tide, her crew were able to walk ashore. Fisher Engineering was awarded the contract to refloat her. Against the advice of Captain Farley of the Garibaldi Life Saving Station, the Fisher engineers off loaded 1,300 tons of ballast, a fatal mistake.

Garibaldi Rescue, April 6, 1913

During high tide, they began the effort to refloat the Mimi. Slowly, the vessel slid from the sand to the ocean. An extraordinarily high wave slammed into her. With no ballast, she was twisted sideways and capsized. Waves pulled crewmen from the deck into the roaring ocean, where they were slammed into twisted spars and broken masts. Fourteen crew drowned. Only the captain, one crew member, and the floater survived, despite the best efforts of the Garibaldi life savers.

The Wreck of the Glenneslin

The square-rigger ship, Glenneslin, was built in Liverpool, England, in 1885. It was an amazing ship. In 1901, she beat a field of eight square-riggers in a trans-ocean race by 17 days. In 1902, she sailed 1,000 miles in four days. She also held a record for sailing from Portland, Oregon, to Port Elizabeth, South Africa, in 74 days.

On October 1, 1913, the Glenesslin was bound for Portland. Suddenly, the vessel turned towards the rolling waters at the base of Mt. Neah-Kah-Nie, north of Manzanita. At 2:30 p.m., the ship crashed into the base of the 1,600-foot mountain.

Captain Williams and the 21 crewmen reached the rocks safely. But rescuers smelled alcohol and thought some of the crew were drunk.

As shown in the photo, the crash was quite a dramatic image. In fact, in the photograph, you can see a second photographer also capturing the image of the ship wreck.

The Court of Inquiry into how the wreck happened captured international attention. After examining the officers and the crew of the wrecked ship, the officers were held responsible for the drunken behavior of their crew. Because the wreck occurred in comparatively clear weather, Captain Williams was charged with being "negligent in his duty."

Breaking waves quickly destroyed the Glenesslin. Some people believed that is was purposely wrecked as part of a nefarious scheme to collect her insured value in a day when the steamer was crowding the square-rigger off the high seas.

After an exhaustive investigation, the insurance was finally paid, the loss being recorded as due to the inexperienced first and second officers who were only 22 years of age.

[Source: Shipwrecks of the Pacific Coast by James A. Gibbs}

BRITISH SHIP "GLENESSLIN"
WRECKED ON NEAH-KAH-NIE'S
SHORE OCT 1, 1913.
PHOTO © BY MAYER.

Cloverdale

Miss Bergetta Nelson
McMinnville, Oregon
This is a dolphin the boys found on the beach. It was seven ft. long three ft. in diameter. Hary is the second to the left. Mae has gone to T.-lo [Tillamook] get her teeth filled and I am staying in her place.
Kitti
Cloverdale

Novocain was introduced to dentistry in 1915, the year this postcard was mailed. It's hard to say if it had made it all the way to Tillamook in time for this woman's fillings. Prior to 1915, ether may have been used, and dentists often used cocaine. Some narcotics were available over the counter in the form of cures and remedies.

CLOVERDALE, OREGON

Dolph, 1915

Named for Senator Dolph, the original site was at a stage coach toll road built by Jordan Fugua, 1878-1882. About a half mile south was another toll road, that followed the Little Nestucka, built by George Baxter. Dolph served as a rest stop with all the necessary accommodations, including a post office. In 1916-1917, a public road was put through, ending the need for a town named Dolph. There is no trace of Dolph left.

Pacific City

Nehalem

Nehalem was chartered in 1899. When this photo [opposite page] was taken, Nehalem asked the federal government to build two jetties at the entrance to the Nehalem Bay. Later, in the 1920s, bridges for rail and car travel were built across the Nehalem River. The Roosevelt Highway (now Highway 101), divides the town into east and west sides. Prior to the establishment of the bridges a small ferry was used to navigate people across the Nehalem River. [For a more detailed history visit the Nehalem website.]

Dear Clair

For once I will write you a letter. I will have a party. I will bring the things over to your house I pay you back for your route card thiar is not enoug room on the card so I will writ a letter.

Mrs. Claire Mc

12139 0th Ave.

From Helen

This card was never mailed.

No 183 Come to Manzanita Beach It's Fine Near Nehalem Oregon.

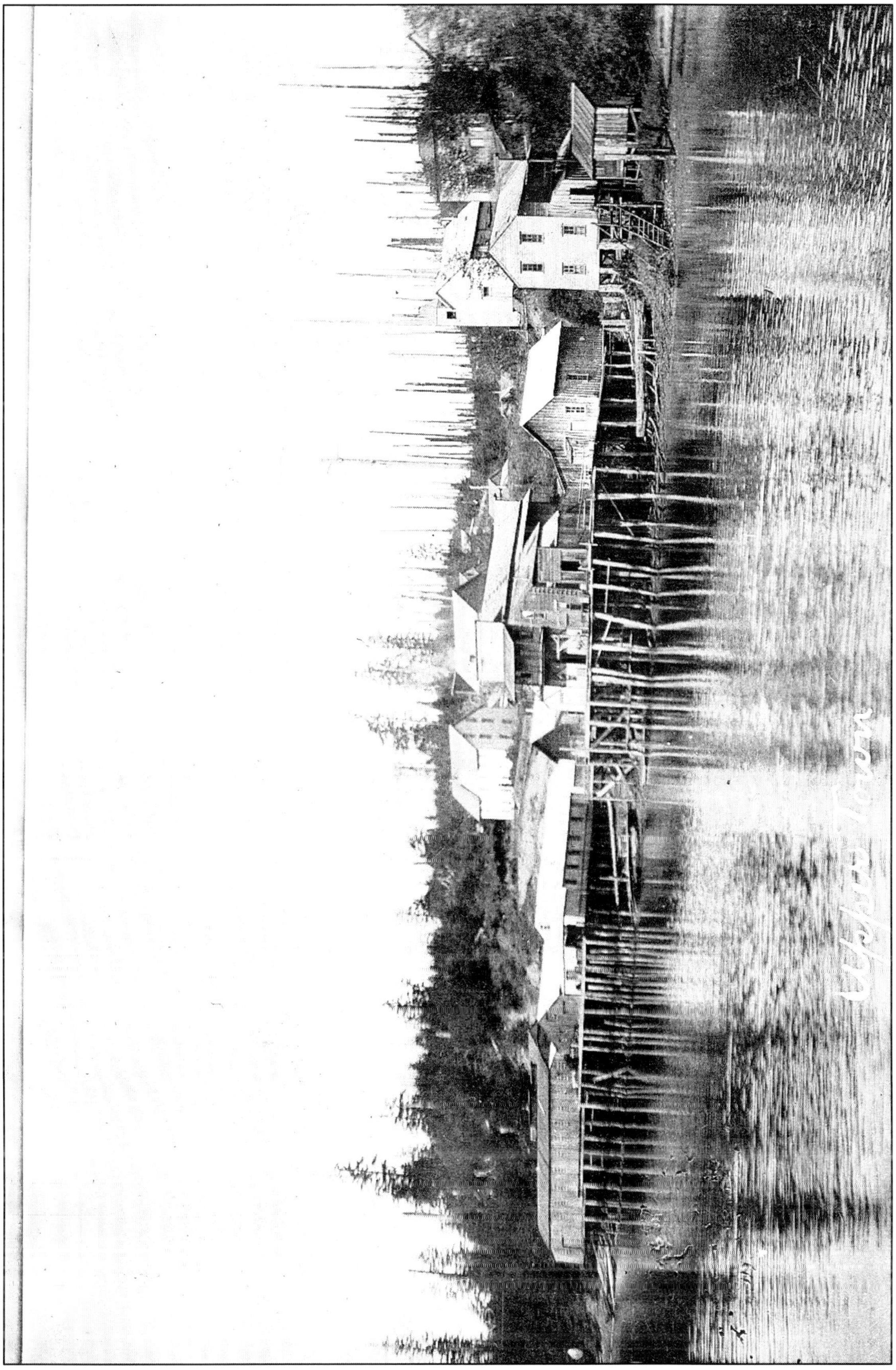
Upper Town

Nehalem, April 27, 1928

Rodney F. Brown
Sunday
Dear Rodney:
Spending the day here we just came down from the mountan has been a glorious day.
El-ohut?
Will write tomorrow

Wheeler

Colman H. Wheeler founded Wheeler in 1910. He opened a sawmill in 1912. WWI gave a huge boost to the economy of Wheeler, Nehalem, and Brighton. By 1918, the Army was involved in harvesting spruce trees. The Army manned the mills and worked the forests, making up for the shortage of able-bodied workers. Very quickly, new rail lines were cut into the forests along with spruce-paved logging roads that were strong enough to hold the heavy trucks of logs.

[For a more detailed history visit the Wheeler website.]

Mr W. White

Clarimont, Calif.

Dear Bro:

Got you a card to let you know I am still alive and feeling fine hope you all are the same.

As ever Bro Jack

Wheeler Oregon

SAW MILL SCENE WHEELER OREGON.

Spruce Brigades

The Spruce Brigades were a part of the Spruce Production Division of the Army Signal Corp and were members of the Loyal Legion of Loggers and Lumbermen, a union to establish support for the war effort.

When the Army arrived on the coast early in 1918, the lumbermen were trying to organize with the help of the Union of Industrial Workers of the World. The Army resolved the differences between mill owners and the lumbermen by establishing the same rules for the mills and loggers as the Signal Corp. The 8-hour work day was one of the benefits. The mill owners didn't like having the Army involved in their businesses, but they did like the stability it brought to the work force.

There were 60 camps established in the Northwest, but not all of them were used because the war ended on the eleventh month, on the eleventh day, on the eleventh hour, 1918.

The Army immediately stopped production! In a very short time, all the equipment purchased by the Army was removed from the mills, sent to Vancouver, and put up for auction.

While this was an abrupt departure, they did leave behind well-developed logging roads, a railroad system extending well into the forests, bars on many of the small bay inlets, and port improvements up and down the Northwest coast line.

[For more information read the "Spruce Brigades" by Rod Crossley.]

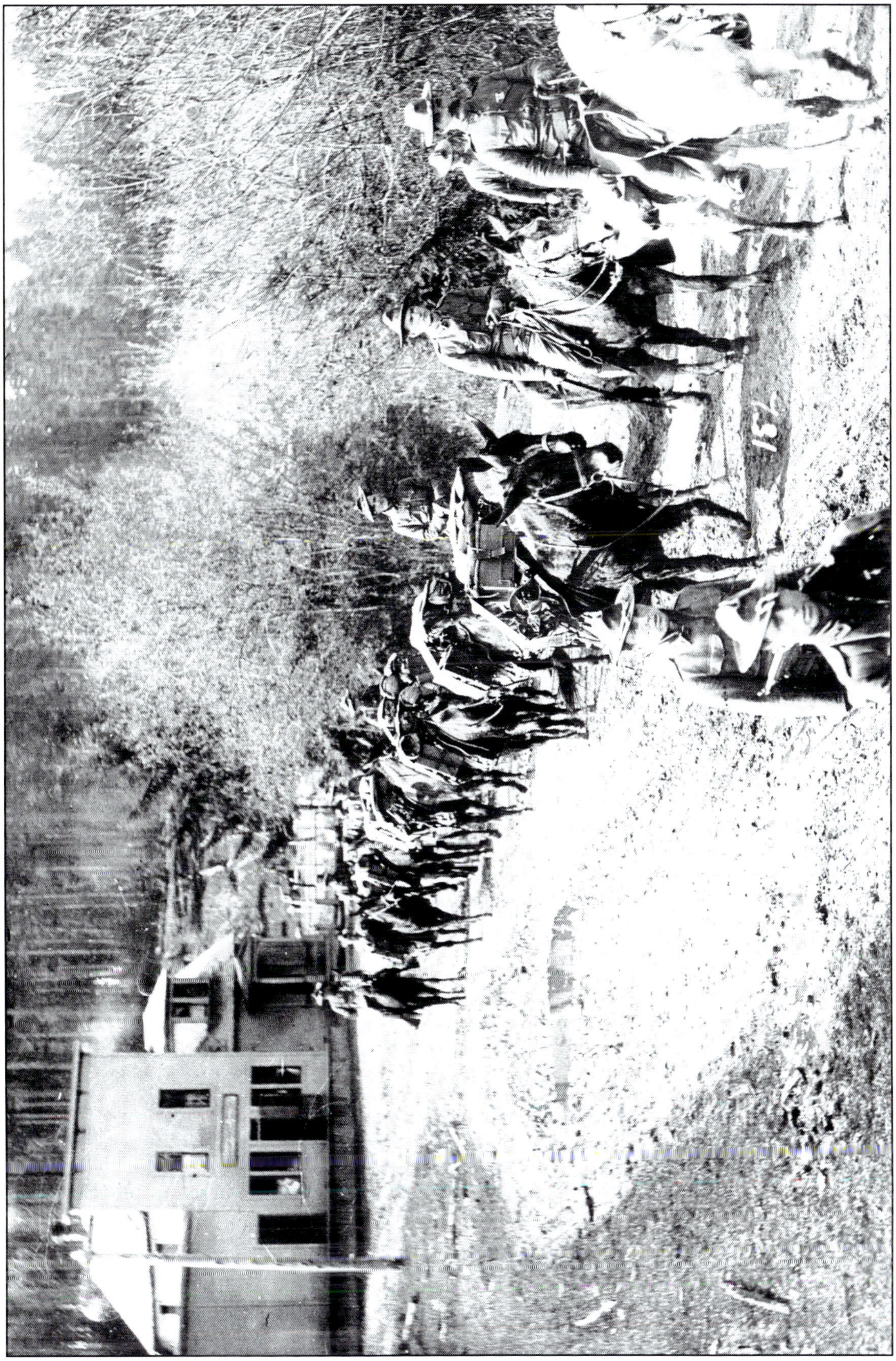

Spruce Brigade loading rail cars near Tillamook

Close Up

"GIGANTIC SPRUCE TREE OREGON — OREGON SPRUCE WILL WIN THE WAR"

Spruce Camp near Newport, Ore.

Taft

This is a view of Taft at the entrance of the Siletz Bay. If the spruce division had activated camp 30 in Siletz, the spruce that would have been harvested and would have left via the Siletz Bay. This is a lot of "would haves" because camp 30, after its establishment and roads were built to service it, was never activated.

Grahams Landing/Toledo

John Graham founded Grahams Landing in 1866. But when the post office was opened in 1868, his son renamed the city "Toledo," because he was homesick for Toledo, Ohio.

When this photograph of downtown Toledo was taken, the Spruce Brigades (Army Signal Corp) was building a mill to harvest spruce wood for the war effort. However, the mill was never finished because the war had ended. Its contents were taken to Vancouver, Washington, for resale. The mill was purchased by private interests and eventually opened and began processing lumber in 1923.

Even though the mill was never finished, it did operate in 1918. World War I ended on November 11, 1918. Therefore, this image was from very early 1918.

Main street of Toledo as you can see the few stores all old and old buildings no improvements at all very old country site it will be some place after this mill get in running order.

Private J.F. [?]
Company 108 Infantry Camp Greene
Charlotte
North Carolina
Toledo Ore. April 16, 1918
My dear Boy I received your letter tonight and was so glad to get it even if it was short. I can't write a letter as I havn't got an envelope. So please excuse me for this time. I am pretty well & so is the rest I worked at Petersons today but I didn't have much to do. I was through at 130 and didn't have to go back until 5. So that isn't so bad. I went and saw some war pictures tonight it sure was interesting. Well dear I will have to close for tonight. Will write a letter tomorrow with love Your Rose

Toledo Football, around 1916-1918

Football in the 1910's was at the outset of the journey into the game we know today. 1905 marked a drastic change in the rules and play of football with an eye toward player safety. Head injuries, broken necks, severe lacerations, and multiple player deaths moved President Teddy Roosevelt and others to meet and change fundamental practices of football. The forward pass was legalized, the punt became part of the game, the wide receiver position was created, and limitations on "unnecessary roughness" were implemented, and the game gradually moved toward a more recognizable form of the game we see today.

By the 1910's a small Catholic University in Indiana was winning games with their mastery of the forward pass, and Notre Dame Football has been an icon of the sport since.

After the turn of the century, high school football and local clubs were gaining in popularity. The new rules allowed parents to feel as though their children would be safer playing the rough and tumble sport. However, helmets were more than 25 years away from being mandated, and facemasks further even than that.

Safety aside, these clubs and high school teams became rallying hubs for the towns and neighborhoods in the United States, with most teams displaying the toughness and resiliency of the place they represented. Football was well on its way to becoming America's favorite spectator sport, and playing the game was a true rite of passage for many young men and boys.

[Basketball and football essays contributed by Robert McAfee, Newport, Oregon.]

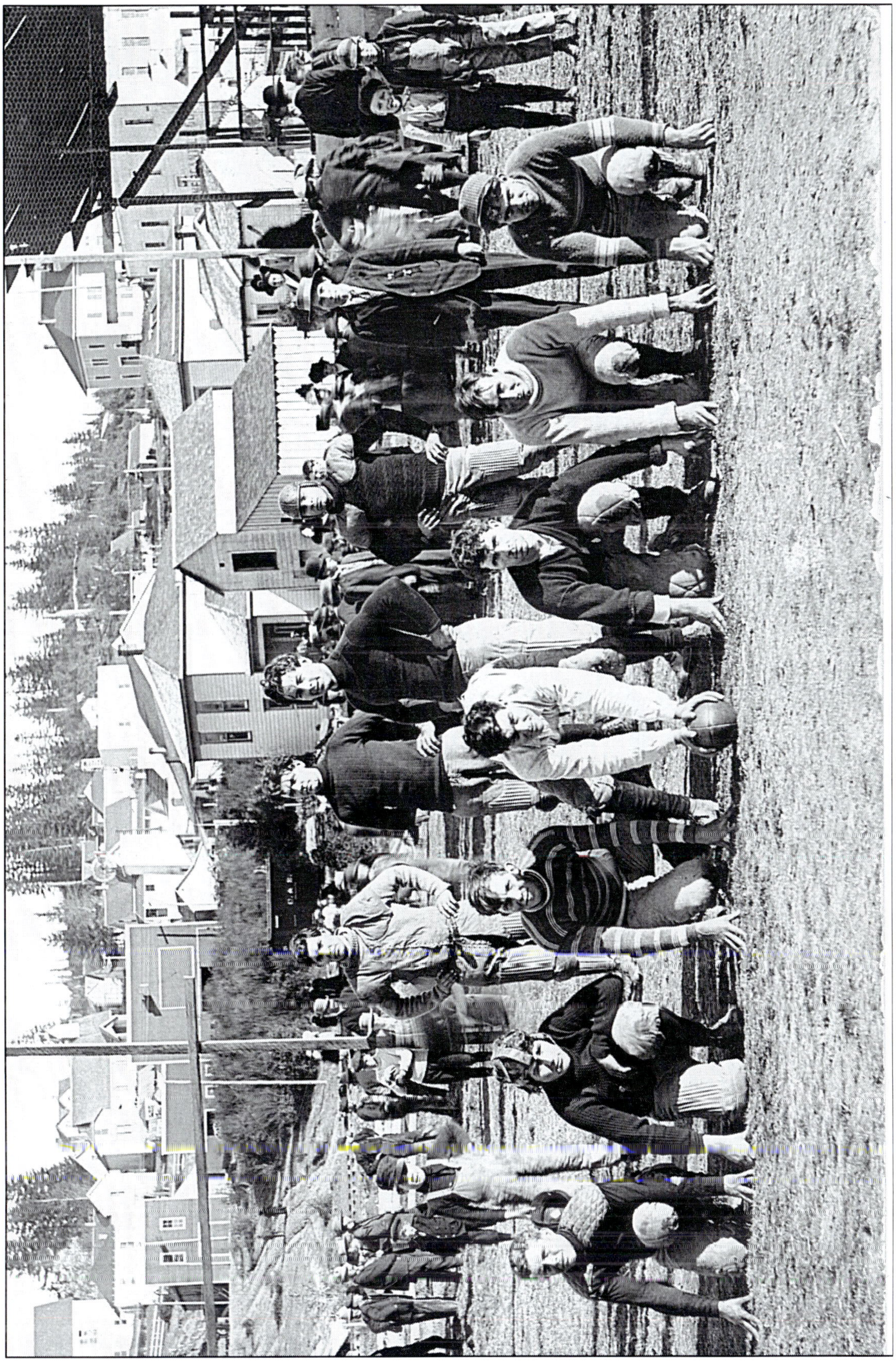

Newport, 1905

533. Bathing Girls at Newport, Oregon.

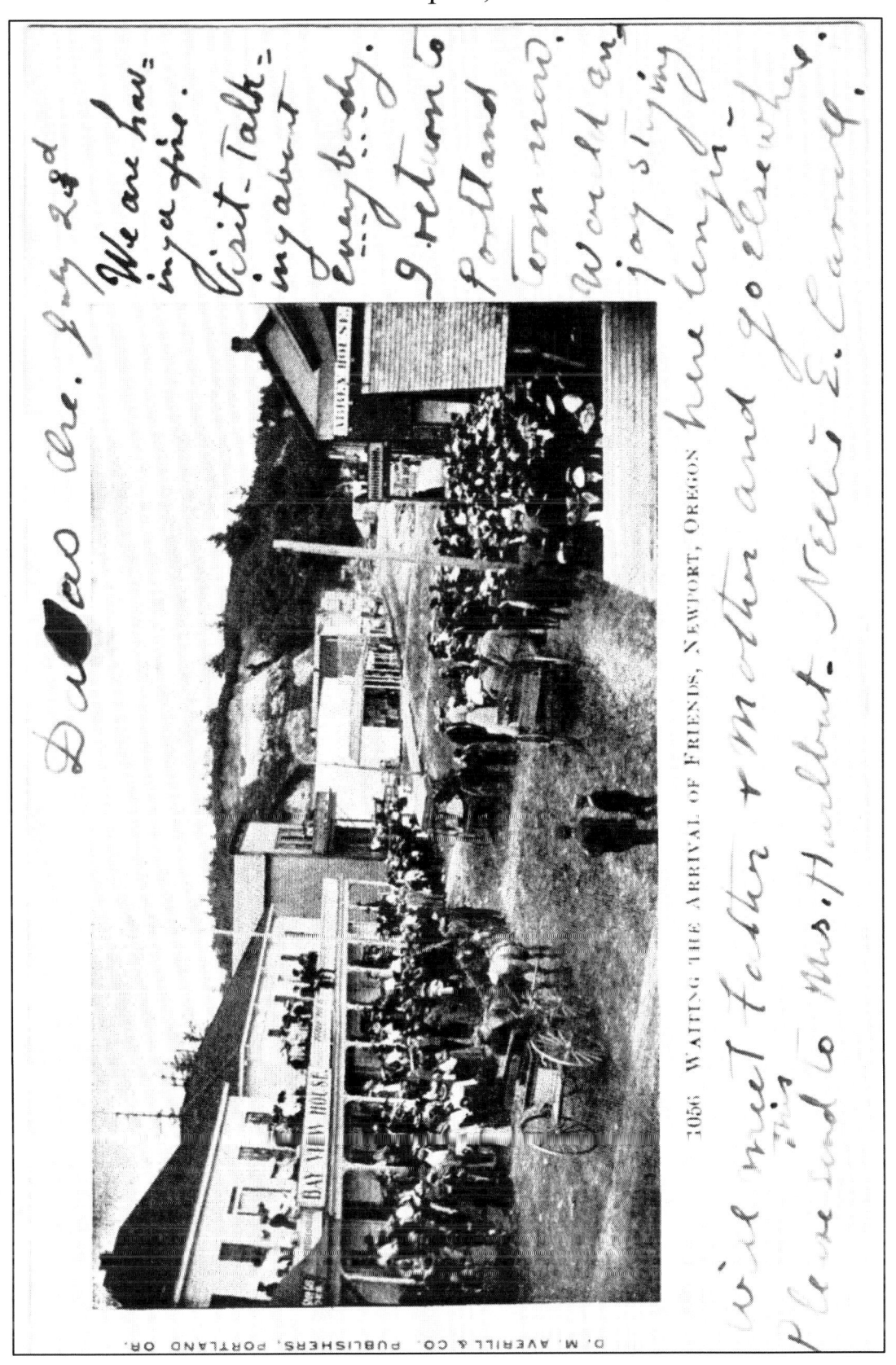

Newport, 1906

Newport, Front Street, 1910

When these photos were taken there was only one way to get to Newport, and that was by water. Shallow draft boats brought travelers from Elk City, then by boat to Newport. If you were coming from up north or from a further southern location, you came over the Yaquina Bay bar by boat. Even when the railroad was completed from Elk City to Yaquina, (originally for the purpose of logging), you still had to board a boat at Yaquina City and travel down river to Newport.

At Newport the final leg of your trip would be a wagon ride over the hill to the real destination for travelers, the resort town of Nye Beach which even at this time had fine hotels and a Natatorium. A north south land route to connect all the small population centers along the coast wasn't conceived (for military purposes) until 1919 which ultimately became Highway 101. (Briefly named the Roosevelt Highway)

Front Street, Newport, Oregon.

Earliest photo of Front Street, looking west, Newport

Note the spruce-paved street in this later photo.

93

Mrs. Mary Yarwood
846 Division St.
Portland, Ore

We are going to the light house about a 5 mile walk today. You should see the fish the men are catching. One of our neighbors gave us some yesterday. We can get clams and ouster, but there is so much to do we haven't had time to get any yet. Guess we will stay 2 weeks. Tell Juollie Hello with love Hattie.

Nye Beach 1918

Note the man in the military uniform talking to the man on horseback.

Newport, Sept. 12, 1913

Hello:—Say aren't you ever coming over here or did you get my card we are getting rich finding agets and "diamonds" it is beautiful weather her but I would like to be there for the Opening of the new Bligh theater Earl is going home tomorrow well be sur and write to me Sometime.   Will be home next Thursday if not before.

Valori

Dear Carl:

We are getting a long nicly hou are you & Johnie making it I furgot to tell you to go & pick my peas to cook also blackberries go & get them when ever you want them.

Your sister Martha

NO 10 A BIRDSEYE VIEW OF NYE BEACH NEAR NEWPORT ORE

Women on balcony of Abbey Hotel.

Abbey Hotel, Newport

Opened in 1911, the Abbey Hotel was proud of having 6 lightening rods on its roof. It burnt down in 1964.

Newport, Sept. 7 1908
I think I'll like it real well we are only in Newport now but we leave very soon Howard and his wife are here so I wont be so lonesome. Don't write till you here from me again. M

Miss Sylvia Leneve
Bandon Ore
Aug. 01, 11 Newport
Sylvia, Paiten came O.K. thank's
So Anna Wiggle Woggle finaly got hers did she. Gee it took her a long time to landine. Well things are about the same with me. Some big get but the season is coming to an end well be good...

DEEP-SEA FISHING ON THE BEAVER.
NEWPORT, ORE.
Aug. 14, 1911.

"Newport Sports."

Gas Schooner Anvil

The gasoline schooner Anvil was built in San Francisco in 1905. It was a 116-foot vessel with 300 horsepower Union gas engines. It worked between Portland, Coos Bay, Bandon, and Yaquina. Passengers traveled in Pullman berths and she carried 300 tons of freight.

She stranded on the north spit of the Siuslaw River on April 11, 1913. Although she was refloated, she was stripped of her engine and most other equipment of value.

This is the boat we came on. It's a dandy to, it rode over those swells fine if it did turn over turns inside out. Ha Ha Etta

Mrs. D.W. Bradham
Springfield Oregon

Dear Friend, Got your letter. Was glad to hear from you will answer soon this is the schooner anvil that was wrecked below Florence near me a few weeks ago. Everybody has seen it but me come down 25th for the annual festival. Answer soon with love Marie.

Train Travel to Newport

The story of how the train made it all the way to Toledo, and then to Yaquina City, is a long one, too long for this book. So here is a brief summary.

On December 18, 1907, the Southern Pacific bought out the Corvallis and Eastern railroad for $750. Under Southern Pacific ownership the name was kept and the line operated for the most part as it did before.

On July 1, 1915, when the Southern Pacific gained total control, plans for an extension into Newport were scrapped when it became apparent the Newport was not going to be the next San Francisco. And Newport did not want a train depot.

However, Newport was heavily advertised as a tourist destination. For $1.50 you could leave Corvallis at 8:20 am, arrive in Yaquina City, hop onto the steamer (junk) "Newport," and continue to the city of Newport. Upon arrival, you could spend a couple of hours at the beach, then catch the steamer "Newport" to Yaquina City, board the train at 6:15 pm, and be in Corvallis at about 11:00 pm.

(Yaquina City no longer exists.)

NO. 9 DEPOT AT YAQUINA ON WAY TO NEWPORT, ORE.

Blakley Family, Newport, Postcards

4-14-14
Mrs. Jas Phillipps
Warsaw, N.Y.
In the old building again got home all right...will write a letter soon have been pretty busy day & night
H.P.B.

[card on opposite page]

Vincent, Mary, Herbert Blakley

"me" Lloyd Blakley in Newport Band at Newport 1916

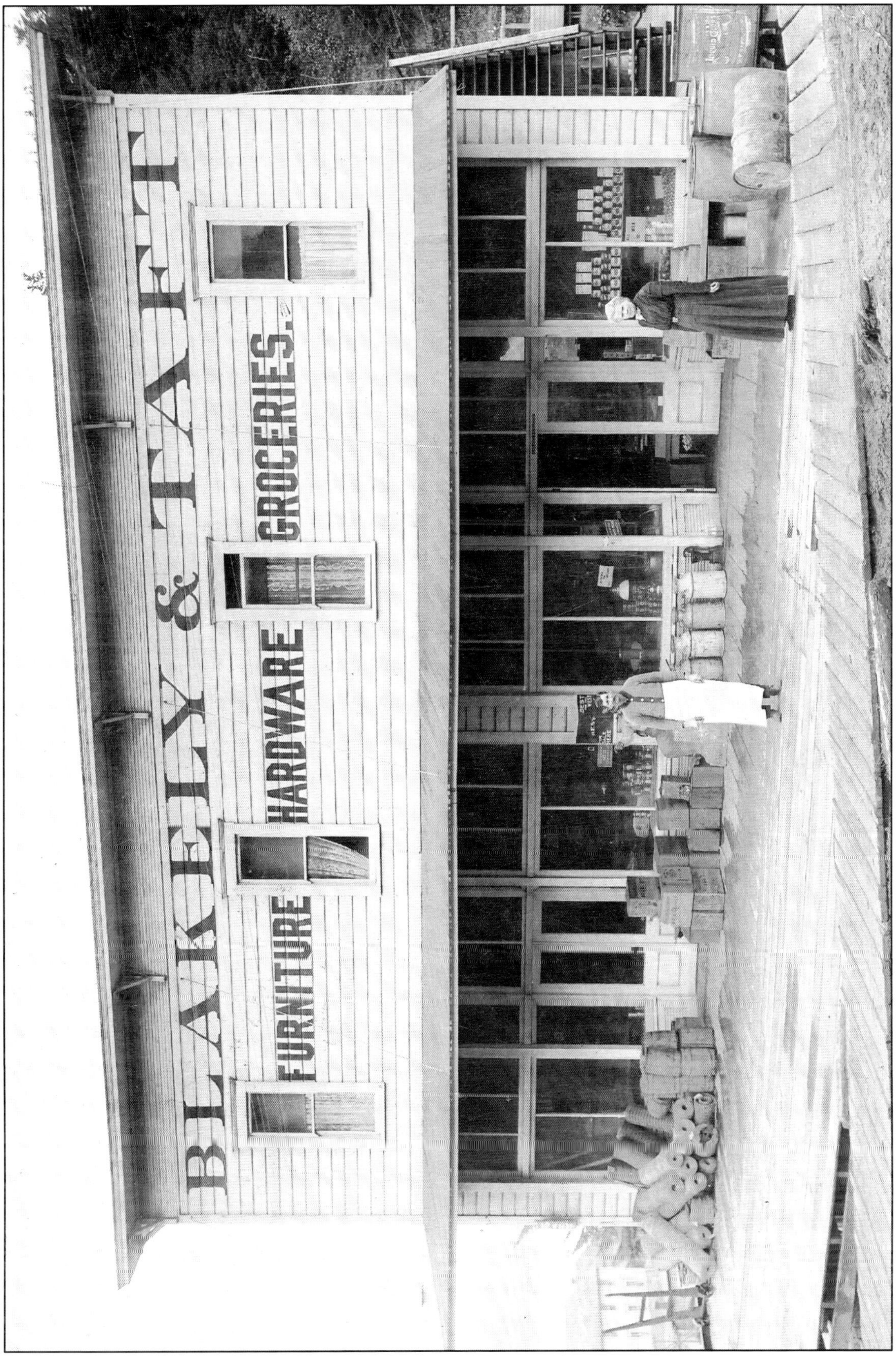
BLAKELY & TAFT
FURNITURE HARDWARE GROCERIES.

Newport, July 26, 1916

Received the card. Have not been in H., except in the evening, lately. Have you taken your vacation? If you come down here let me know. Am having a lovely time will stay until first of the next week. Sincerely Lucille

John Ayers
Bloomingdale Mich
Dear Friends:
Was very glad to get your letter. We are over here on the Pacific for a week. Came across from Yaquina to Newport on this boat. This is a fine place. Roland is having a fine time fishing and bathing. Hope to hear from you again. Write to Albany. Love to all Emma

105. CAPE FOULWEATHER LIGHT HOUSE & KEEPERS HOME NEAR AGATE BEACH

Newport

7-2-1921

My very dear Kath

Just finished breakfast & then came a knock at the door & my boots were handed to me by mail. Thanks dear very much as I expect to soon put them to use but you did not send me the heavy socks that were with them however these will do very much I expect as I shall double up. I did not find any letter in the boots socks papers? & I have not heard from in 2 days. Tell Rod I have a tale to tell about beans but will leave it until I write tomorrow. I miss the dear girl very much but am going [?] tomorrow.

Love to all many thanks Daddy

Ines St. Looking East. Newport. Ore.

Elk City

Originally named Newton, (then renamed Elk City after big Elk Creek, in 1888) came to be in 1866 by the Yaquina Wagon Road Co. Elk City started with a store and warehouse. Within a year the city had another store, a hotel, and church/school house, and, eventually, a mill. A post office was established in 1868. Boats regularly traveled up stream on the Yaquina River, to gather mail to be distributed downstream as it was the terminus of the land route into the area at that time. The railroad arrived in the late 19th century, eventually connecting Elk City with Corvallis, Albany, and Yaquina.

The 20th century took its toll on small inland communities. The post office closed in 1958, and Elk City became a ghost town and camp ground with 12 camp sites and boat ramp. Yaquina no longer exists.

Ballground Elk City, Ore.

Elk City, Ore. 447

Waldport Camp

Mr. Ernest E Mitchell
Arlington, Mass.

Dear Ernest,
This is a picture of our camp at the Pacific Ocean. We were so near the beach, that the spray kept our tents wet most of the time. We are well, hope you are. Write when you can with love Hank and Cynthia

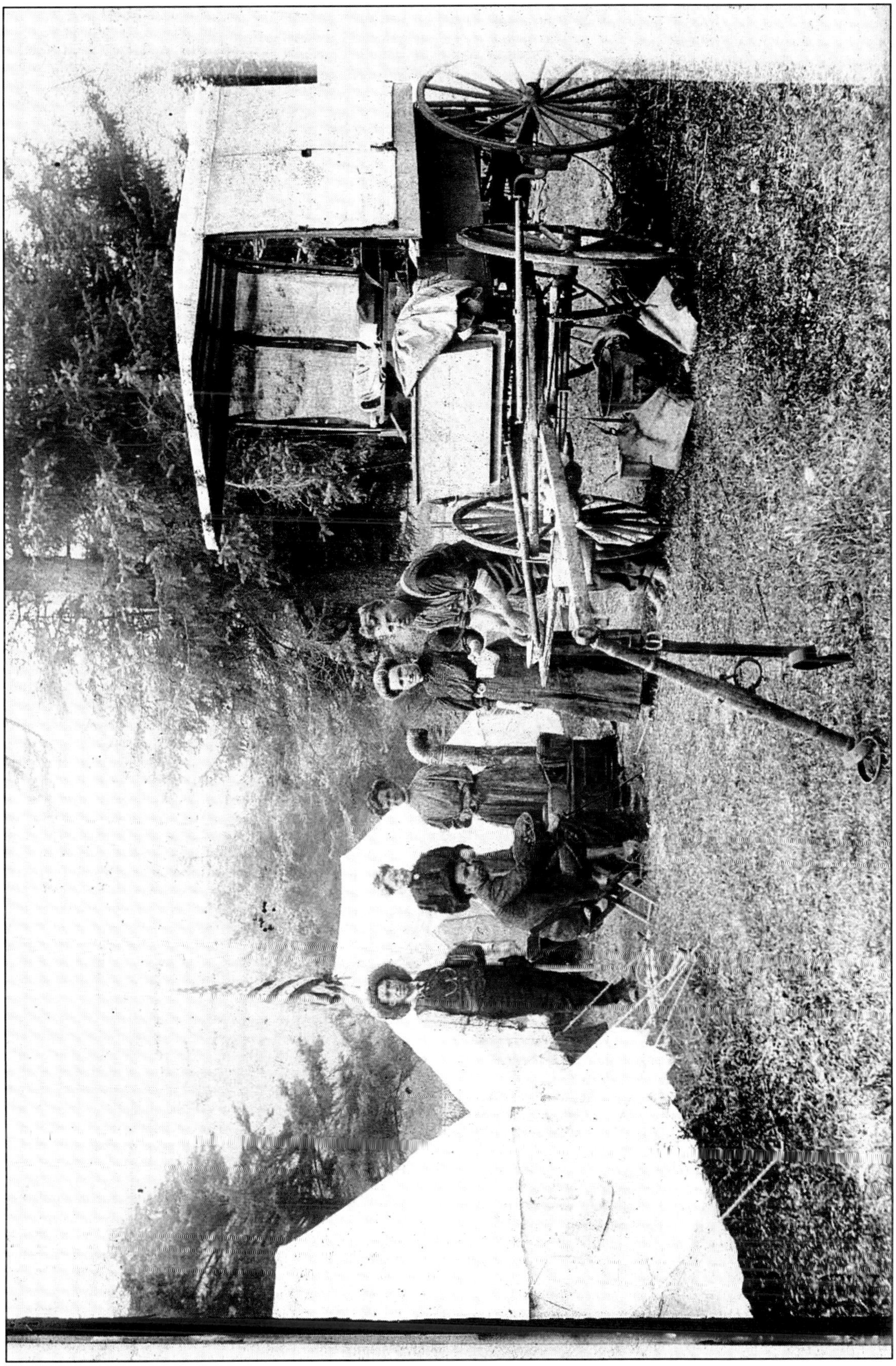

Waldport

Waldport was incorporated in 1911. This card was mailed in 1909 by the photographer who took the picture. In 1909, the telephone was creeping its way up the coast from Yachats. It would be another nine years before the Spruce Brigades (Army Signal Corp) would build the first mills to process spruce, and build the first road to Toledo to process the lumber. Living was not easy. Most people grew vegetables in yard gardens, and took advantage of the hunting, digging clams, and fishing for protein. Goods and services were brought in and taken out over the Alsea Bay bar by shallow draft steamers.

[For a more detailed history go the Waldport website.]

Walport, August 22, 1911

Sylvia

This our area of the village near which I live, this my own work as I have a camera and like to do photographie work. I cannot obtain views like those you sent me. They were beautiful this is a picturesque country new but improving right on the Pacific coast. Yours is old and well settled isn't it?

Your post card friend (Waldport Ore)

Edgar

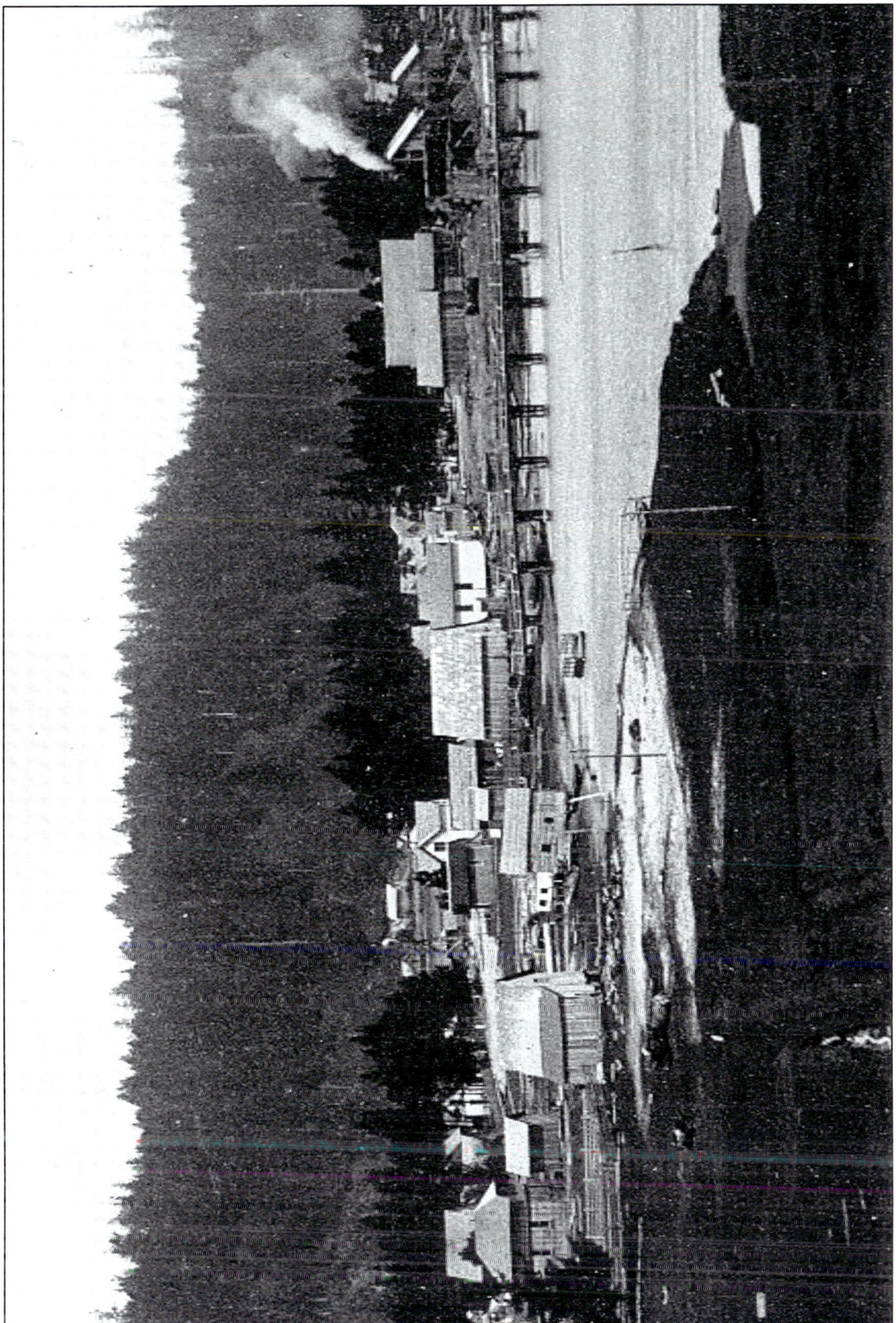

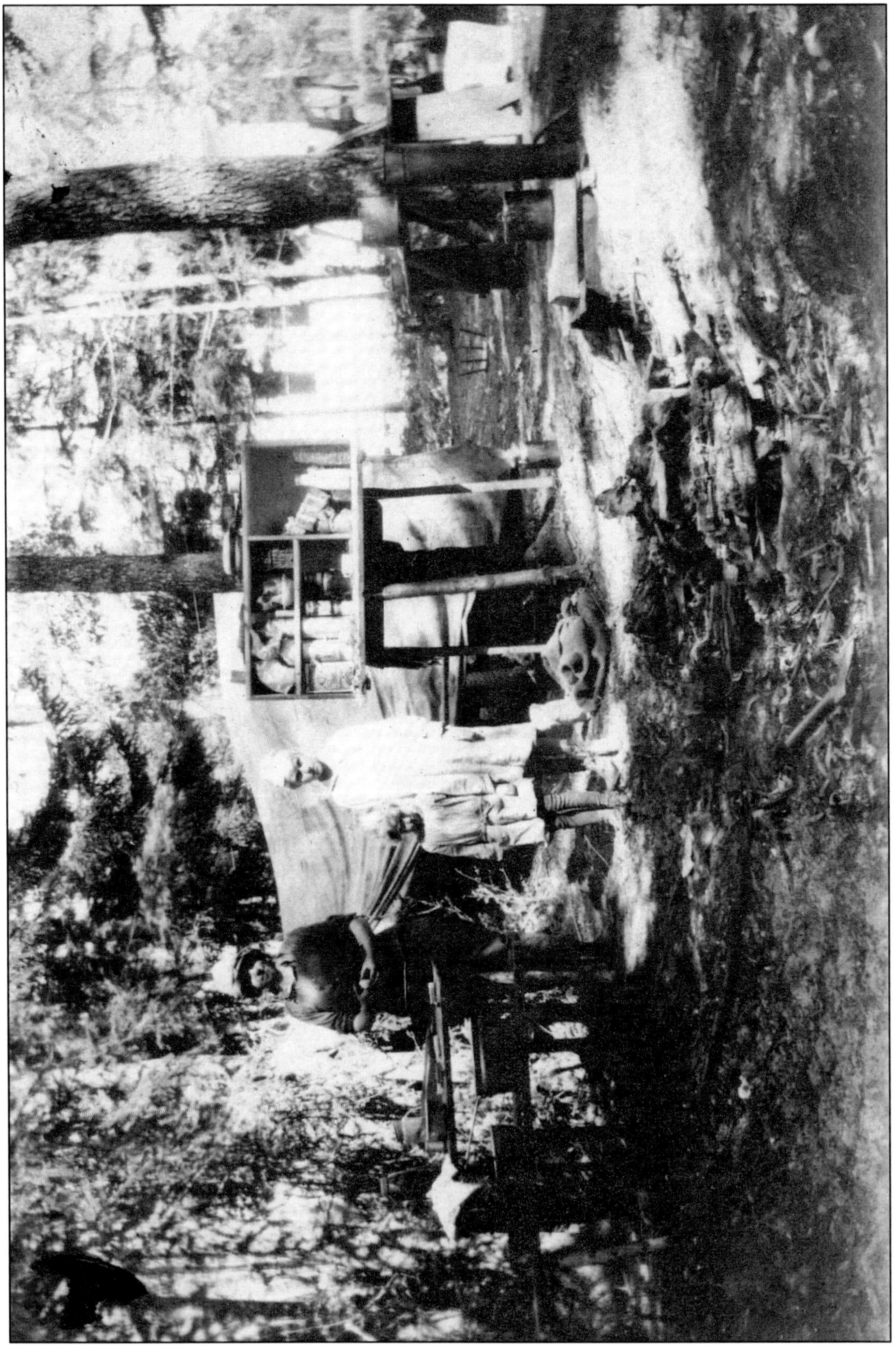

Epilogue

My hometown is Tillamook and I moved to Newport over 30 years ago. Learning the area's history through finding postcards has been an exciting adventure. And rather than quench my thirst for historical information, it's made stopping, so I can share my treasures, difficult.

If there are any errors in the information presented, please let me know. (Write to Mary@Webster.org) I want to be as accurate as possible.

Contact info to purchase books:

Multiple copy discounts are available.

Mary@Webster.org

Made in United States
North Haven, CT
30 October 2022